Beauty

Wildflowers and Flowering Shrubs of the
Southern Interior of British Columbia

Neil L. Jennings

Rocky
Mountain Books
VANCOUVER • VICTORIA • CALGARY

Rocky Mountain Books
#108 – 17665 66A Avenue
Surrey, BC V3S 2A7
www.rmbooks.com

Rocky Mountain Books
PO Box 468
Custer, WA
98240-0468

Library and Archives Canada Cataloguing in Publication

Jennings, Neil L
Central beauty : wildflowers and flowering shrubs of the southern
interior of British Columbia / Neil L. Jennings.
Includes index.

ISBN 978-1-897522-03-5

1. Wild flowers–British Columbia–Identification.
2. Flowering shrubs–British Columbia–Identification.
I. Title.

QK203.B7J46 2008   582.1309711   C2007-907289-5

Library of Congress Control Number: 2007943348

Edited by Joe Wilderson
Proofread by Corina Skavberg
Interior design by John Luckhurst
All cover and interior photos supplied by Neil L. Jennings except as
otherwise noted

Printed and bound in Hong Kong

Rocky Mountain Books gratefully acknowledges the financial support of the
Government of Canada through the Book Publishing Industry Development
Program (BPIDP); the Canada Council for the Arts; and the province of British
Columbia through the British Columbia Arts Council and the Book Publishing
Tax Credit for our publishing activities.

This book has been produced on 100% post-consumer recycled paper,
processed chlorine free and printed with vegetable-based dyes.

Acknowledgements

When I commenced work on this book, I was aware that I would need assistance in obtaining photographs of many of the included species. In that regard I contacted a number of wildflower photographers who were known to me, and some who were perfect strangers. Their generous support was heartening, and, indeed, without it the project could not have been completed in the timeframe desired. Heartfelt thanks go to the photographers who generously and graciously permitted me to use some of their work in the book: Anne Elliott of Calgary, Alberta; Dave Ingram of Courtenay, British Columbia; Tracy Utting of Iqaluit, Nunavut; Gill Ross of Okotoks, Alberta; Werner Eigelsreiter of Oliver, British Columbia; and Jim Riley of Randle, Washington. Particular thanks also go to Virginia and Doug Skilton of Surrey, British Columbia, who not only generously contributed photographs but also were also extraordinarily forthcoming with advice and assistance on the completion of the book. I also want to tip my hat to Rose Klinkenberg who administers E-Flora BC (www.eflora.bc.ca), which website provided me with a tremendous amount of research information while compiling the book. Lastly, I want to thank my wife, Linda, for her support, encouragement, patience, and companionship in our past and future outings.

This book is dedicated to my children – Shawn, Jenise, Matthew, and Simon – all of whom put up with my wildflower passion, often even aiding and abetting it. Thanks for that. I am enormously proud of each of you.

CONTENTS

INTRODUCTION

This book is intended to be a field guide for the amateur naturalist to the identification of wild flowering plants commonly found in the southern interior areas of British Columbia. This is not a book for scientists. It is a book for the curious traveller who wants to become acquainted with the flowers encountered during outings. This book differs from most other field guides in that it has large, clear photographs of the species treated; it makes no assumption that the reader has a background in things botanical – as seems to be assumed in many other guides; and it is small enough to actually carry in the field and not be a burden. I believe that most people want to be able to identify the flowers they encounter because that ability enriches their outdoor experience. Some might think it a difficult skill to perfect, but take heart and consider this: you can easily put names and faces together for several hundred family members, friends, acquaintances, movie stars, authors, business and world leaders, sports figures, etc. Wildflower recognition is not different from that, and it need not be complicated.

For purposes of this book, the area of interest is loosely defined as the portions of British Columbia that lie east of the crests of the coastal mountains, west of the crests of the Rocky Mountains, and south of the boreal forest – very roughly an east/west line drawn at about the position of Williams Lake, British Columbia. The southern limit of the area extends well into the states of Washington, Idaho, and Montana. Plants do not recognize man-made boundaries, and overlap occurs. The floral community of the coastal areas of British Columbia, Washington, and Oregon are not addressed, owing to the limitations of space available in the book. Indeed, this book would virtually double in size – and weight – if that floral community were included. The coastal floral community is addressed in my book *Coastal Beauty: Wildflowers and Flowering Shrubs of Coastal British Columbia and Vancouver Island,* also published by Rocky Mountain Books.

This book does not cover all of the species of wildflowers and flowering shrubs that exist in the area, but it does cover a large representation of the floral community that might be encountered in a typical day during the blooming season. No book that I am acquainted with covers all species in the region, and indeed if such a book existed, it would be a tome that could not be casily carried. For example, it is estimated that in the Composite Family (Sunflowers) alone there are hundreds of species in over 100 genera in the area. Obviously, space will not permit a discussion of all such species, nor would it be pertinent for the amateur naturalist. The region harbours a vast diversity of habitat, including dry plateaus, arid basins, wet mountainous zones, and the Rocky Mountain Trench.

"Do you know what this flower is called?" is one of the most often asked questions when I meet people in the field. Hopefully, this book will enable the user to answer the question. Identification of the unknown species is based on comparison of the unknown plant with the photographs contained in the book, augmented by the narrative descriptions associated with the species pictured in the book. In many cases the exact species will be apparent, while in other cases the reader will be led to plants that are similar to the unknown plant, thus providing a starting point for further investigation. I believe that most people will have a richer experience outdoors if they learn to recognize the wildflowers they encounter. For the purposes of this book, scientific jargon has been kept to a minimum. I have set out to produce the best photographic representations I could obtain, together with some information about the plant that the reader might find interesting and that might assist the reader in remembering the names of the plants. What I am attempting to do is assist people who want to be able to recognize and identify common wildflowers they see while outdoors. I have tried to keep it simple, while making it interesting and enjoyable. In my view, what most people really want to know about wildflowers is "what is this thing?" and "tell me something interesting about it." Botanical detail, while interesting and enlightening to some of us, will turn off many people.

The plants depicted in the book are arranged first by colour, and then by family. This is a logical arrangement for the non-botanist because the first thing a person notes about a flower is its colour. All of the plants shown in the book are identified by their prevailing common names. Where I knew of other common names applied to any plant, I noted them. I have also included the scientific names of the plants. This inclusion is made to promote specificity. Common names vary significantly from one geographic area to another; scientific names do not. If you want to learn the scientific names of the plants to promote precision, fine. If you do not want to deal with that, fine. Just be mindful that many plants have different common names applied to them depending on geography and local usage.

A few cautionary comments and suggestions:

While you are outdoors, go carefully among the plants so as not to damage or disturb them. In parks, stay on the established trails. In large measure, those trails exist to allow us to view the natural environment without trampling it to death. Many environments are delicate and can be significantly damaged by indiscriminately tromping around in the flora.

Do not pick the flowers. Leave them for others to enjoy. Bear in mind that in national, provincial, and state parks it is illegal to pick any flowers.

Do not attempt to transplant wild plants. Such attempts are most often doomed to failure, and such practices can have devastating consequences for wild stocks.

Do not eat any plants or plant parts. To do so presents a potentially significant health hazard. Many of the plants are poisonous – some violently so.

Do not attempt to use any plants or plant parts for medicinal purposes. To do so presents a potentially significant health hazard. Many of the plants are poisonous – some violently so.

One final cautionary note: the pursuit of wildflowers can be addictive, though not hazardous to your health.

Neil L. Jennings
Calgary, Alberta

PLANT SHAPES AND FORMS

Parts of a Leaf

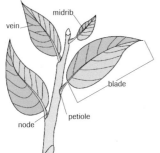

Parts of a Flower

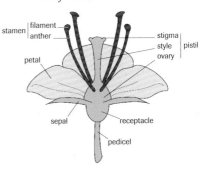

Leaf Arrangements

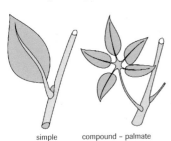

simple   compound – palmate   compound – pinnate   compound – doubly pinnate

Stem Arrangements

opposite   alternate   whorled

Leaf Shapes

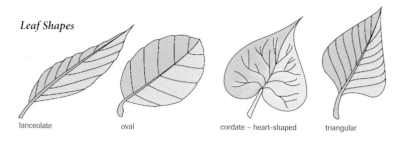

lanceolate   oval   cordate – heart-shaped   triangular

Leaf Margins

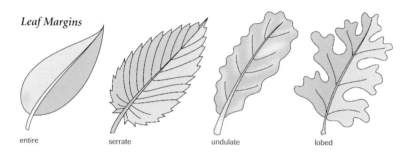

entire   serrate   undulate   lobed

Venation

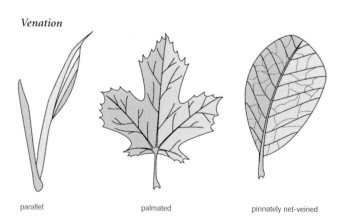

parallel   palmated   pinnately net-veined

TERRITORIAL RANGE OF WILDFLOWERS

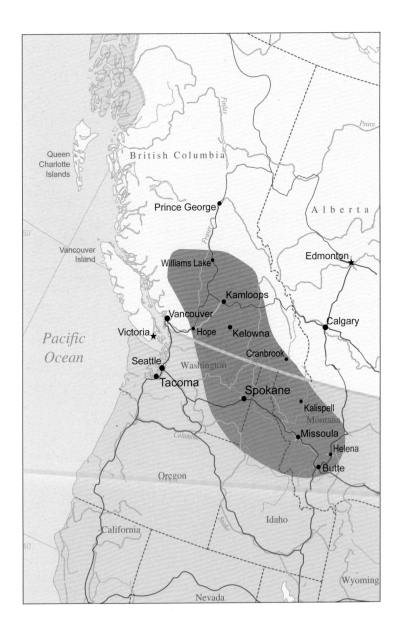

Yellow Flowers

This section includes flowers that are predominantly yellow when encountered in the field. The colour varies from bright yellow to pale cream. Some of the flowers in this section have other colour variations and you might have to check other sections of the book to find the flower. For example, the Paintbrushes (*Castilleja* sp) have a yellow variation, but they are most often encountered in a red colour and they have been pictured in that section for purposes of sorting.

Skunk Cabbage (Yellow Arum)
Lysichiton americanum

ARUM FAMILY

This early-blooming distinctive perennial grows in large patches from a fleshy rhizome, and inhabits swamps, bogs, marshes, and mucky ground at low to middle elevations. The inflorescence appears before the leaves. The inflorescence consists of hundreds of tiny, greenish-yellow flowers sunk into a thick, fleshy stalk known as a spadix, which is surrounded by a large, bright yellow sheath leaf known as a spathe. The broadly elliptic leaves are huge, growing up to 120 cm long on stout stalks. Though it does not actually smell of skunk, the whole plant has an earthy odour, giving rise to the common name. The scent attracts beetles as pollinators.

The genus name, *Lysichiton*, is derived from the Greek *lysis*, which means "loosening," and *chiton*, which means "tunic," a reference to the spathe unfolding from around the spadix. The plant contains needle-like crystals of calcium oxalate which will pierce the lining in the mouth, but those crystals are eliminated when the roots are dried or roasted. Native peoples dried and roasted the plant, then ground it into a flour. The large leaves were used as liners in food-steaming pits and baskets, and as a wrapping material for other foods. The plant is also locally called Swamp Lantern, a reference to the large yellow spathe standing out amidst the dark green background of its preferred habitat. Bears also eat the whole plant, and deer browse on the leaves. The plant is related to taro.

Oregon Grape
Mahonia nervosa (formerly *Berberis nervosa*)

BARBERRY FAMILY

This evergreen shrub is widespread and common at low to middle elevations in dry plateaus and dry to moist forests and openings in the foothills. The plant very closely resembles holly, with shiny, sharp-pointed leaves that turn to lovely orange and rusty colours in the fall. The flowers are pale to bright yellow, round, and bloom in the early spring, giving way to a small purple berry that resembles a grape.

The genus name, *Mahonia*, honours 18th-century Irish-born horticulturist Bernard M'Mahon, who moved to Pennsylvania in 1796 to start a nursery. The specific name, *nervosa*, means "having distinct veins or nerves," a reference to the leaves of the plant. Plants in the genus were once classified in genus *Berberis*, which was the Latinized form of the Arabic name for the barberry fruit. The fruits are very bitter tasting from the plant, but make a delicious jelly when processed. Native peoples extracted a bright yellow pigment from the inner bark and roots of the plant, and used it to dye basket material. The inner bark was also used for medicinal purposes, including easing child delivery, healing wounds, combating infections, and treating venereal disease. Tall Oregon Grape (*M. aquifolium*) is a similar plant in the region, but it grows to much larger sizes than does this species. Its flowers, fruits, and leaves are virtually identical to those of this species.

Common Bladderwort
Utricularia vulgaris

BLADDERWORT FAMILY

This aquatic carnivorous plant is found in shallow water in sloughs, lakes, ditches, and ponds. It floats beneath the surface of the water, with a tangle of coarse stems and leaves. The long, branching, submerged stems have finely divided leaves that spread out like small nets. Attached to the leaves hang numerous small bladders that are actually traps for aquatic insects. When an insect swims into the bladders, small hairs are tripped, which shuts the bladder, trapping the insect inside. The insects are then digested, providing a source of nitrogen for the plant. The yellow flowers appear on leafless stalks that extend above the surface of the water. The corolla of the flower is two-lipped, with brown stripes on the throat. The floral tube extends into a short, spur-like sac at the base.

The genus name, *Utricularia*, is derived from the Latin *utriculus*, which means "small bottle" or "little bag," a reference to the bladders on the plants. The species name, *vulgaris*, means "common."

Blazing Star (Giant Blazing Star)
Mentzelia laevicaulis

BLAZING STAR FAMILY

Virginia Skilton image

This spectacular plant grows up to 1 m tall, and occurs in arid basins and dry grasslands, from valleys to montane elevations. Stiff, barbed, grey hairs cover the angular stems and foliage of the plant. The leaves are up to 30 cm long, lance-shaped, and deeply lobed, with wavy margins. The flowers occur at the top of stout, satiny, white stems. The lemon yellow flowers are large and star-like, with five lance-shaped petals that are up to 8 cm long, and numerous long yellow stamens that burst forth in a fountain-like display. The five outer stamens have expanded, showy filaments, and alternate with the true petals, giving the appearance that the flower has ten petals.

The genus name, *Mentzelia*, honours Christian Mentzel, a 17th-century German botanist. The species name, *laevicaulis*, means "smooth stemmed," which is puzzling, because the stem of this plant is anything but smooth, with its barbed hairs. The plant was first described in the journals of David Douglas, a 19th-century Scottish botanist who did a number of botanical explorations in western North America. Some Native peoples used the root of this plant in a number of medicinal preparations for fevers and a large variety of other ailments. Another member of the *Mentzelia* genus, Evening Star (*M. decapetala*), occurs in prairie habitats. It has large, white flowers, and only blooms at night.

5

Puccoon (Lemonweed)
Lithospermum ruderale

BORAGE FAMILY

A coarse perennial up to 50 cm tall, this plant is firmly anchored to dry slopes and grasslands by a large, woody taproot. The numerous leaves are sharp-pointed, lance-shaped, and clasp the stem. The small yellow flowers are partly hidden in the axils of the leaves near the top of the plant, and have a strong, pleasant scent. The stems and leaves are covered in long white hairs. The fruit is an oval, cream-coloured nutlet that is somewhat pitted, and resembles pointed teeth.

The genus name, *Lithospermum*, is derived from the Greek *lithos*, meaning "stone," and *sperma*, meaning "seed," a reference to the fruit of the plant. Indeed, another common name for the plant is Stoneseed. For centuries, some Native peoples used an extract of the plant for birth control. Natural estrogens in the plant suppress the release of certain hormones required for ovulation. The roots of the plant were used as a source of red dye. Another common name for the plant is Woolly Gromwell. A similar plant, Narrow-Leaved Puccoon (*L. incisum*) appears in the southeastern part of the region. It differs from this species in that the flowers are larger and the petals are fringed or toothed, not smooth like this species.

Yellow Buckwheat (Umbrella Plant)
Eriogonum flavum

BUCKWHEAT FAMILY

This fuzzy haired, tufted perennial favours dry, often sandy or rocky outcrops, eroded slopes, and badlands. The leaves are dark green on top, but appear white to felty on the underside due to the dense hairs. The yellow flowers occur in compound umbels — umbrella shaped clusters — atop the stem. The common name, Umbrella Plant, is testimony to the shape of the inflorescence.

The genus name, *Eriogonum*, is derived from the Greek *erion*, meaning "wool," and *gonu*, meaning "knee or joint," a reference to the hairy or woolly joints of some members of the genus. *Flavum* is Latin meaning "golden yellow." The plant has an unpleasant smell, but the nectar is relished by bees, and produces a strongly flavoured buckwheat-like honey.

Creeping Buttercup
Ranunculus repens

BUTTERCUP FAMILY

This European invader spreads over the ground by slender, creeping stems or runners, similar to those of the Wild Strawberry. The leaf blades are long-stalked, egg- or heart-shaped, and have scalloped margins. The plant is found in moist meadows, on stream banks, and at the margins of lakes and ponds.

Buttercups are among the oldest of flower families, having existed for millions of years before earliest man developed, and are considered one of the most primitive plant families. The cell structure on the petals is such that there is air in the cell vacuoles, and this is responsible for the "whiteness" seen on the petals. The genus name, *Ranunculus*, is from the Greek *rana*, which means "frog," a likely reference to the wetland or marshy habitat of many species in the family. The species name, *repens*, is Latin for "creeping," exactly descriptive of this plant. It has now extended its range from coast to coast and even into Alaska and the Yukon Territory.

Meadow Buttercup
Ranunculus acris

BUTTERCUP FAMILY

This species is a European import that has widely established itself in the region. It grows from fibrous roots, stands up to 80 cm tall, and may have multiple stems. The leaves are hairy, heart-shaped, and deeply lobed almost to the base. The flowers are glossy and yellow, and appear singly or in loose clusters atop hairy stalks.

The origin of the genus name, *Ranunculus*, is explained in the note on Creeping Buttercup (*R. repens*), shown on page 8. The species name, *acris* refers to the acrid juice of the plant. As a general rule, Buttercups contain alkaloids, and some species are poisonous to livestock. In fact, some Native peoples rubbed projectile points with juices from Buttercups to make them poisonous. According to Irish folklore, a cow's milk production would be enhanced if its udder was massaged with Buttercups — a proposition that is probably specious at best.

Sagebrush Buttercup
Ranunculus glaberrimus

BUTTERCUP FAMILY

This beautiful little buttercup is one of the earliest blooming wildflowers in the region, with its bright yellow, shiny petals peeping out from the dead winter grasses of early spring on arid hillsides. The leaves are mainly basal, and elliptic to lance-shaped. The flowers appear in patches or as single blooms.

The origin of the genus name, *Ranunculus*, is discussed in the note on Creeping Buttercup (*R. repens*), shown on page 8. The species name, *glaberrimus*, is Latin meaning "very smooth" or "smoothest," most probably a reference to the shiny, hairless leaves. Sagebrush Buttercups are poisonous, containing an acrid alkaloid, and some Native tribes warned their children not to touch or pick them. Some Natives peoples used the flower as a source of poison for their arrows.

Yellow Columbine
Aquilegia flavescens

BUTTERCUP FAMILY

Lemon yellow in colour, these beautiful flowers nod at the ends of slender stems that lift the flowers above the leaves. Each flower is composed of five wing-shaped sepals, and five tube-shaped petals that are flaring at the open end and tapering to a distinctive spur at the opposite end. The leaves are mainly basal, have long stems, and are deeply lobed. The plant occurs on rock slides, talus slopes, and in meadows in the alpine and subalpine zones.

The origin of the genus name, *Aquilegia*, and the common name Columbine, are discussed in the note on Red Columbine (*A. formosa*), shown on page 232. Where the range of this plant and Red Columbine overlap, they may hybridize to produce flowers with pink-tinged sepals. Some Native peoples looked upon Columbines as good luck charms in gambling and love affairs. A decoction made from the plants was also used as a head wash.

Brittle Prickly-Pear Cactus
Opuntia fragilis

CACTUS FAMILY

This easily recognized plant is prostrate and can form mats on dry, exposed slopes in eroded areas and badlands, often growing on sandy or rocky soil. The stems are flattened and broad, and are covered with clusters of hard, sharp spines that have tufts of sharp bristles at the base. The flowers are large and showy, with numerous yellow petals that are waxy and up to 5 cm long. The fruits are pear-shaped, spiny berries which are edible and often browsed by antelope.

The genus name, *Opuntia*, is derived from the Greek name used by Pliny for a different plant that grew near the town of Opus in Greece. The species name, *fragilis*, is Latin for "brittle" or "fragile," and is most probably a reference to the fact that segments of the plant are easily broken off. Native peoples roasted and ate the plant stems after removing the spines and outer skin. The juices inside the stem were often used as an emergency water supply. The plant contains calcium, phosphorus, and vitamin C, and is said to taste of cucumber. Prairie Prickly-Pear Cactus (*O. polyacantha*) is a closely related species that occurs in the dry plateaus, grasslands, and sagebrush slopes of the southern part of the region and areas east. It is generally a larger plant and has flat, joints between the stems. The flowers are very similar to Brittle Prickly-Pear Cactus. Cactus is derived from the Greek *kaktos*, which means "prickly plant."

Black Sanicle (Snakeroot)
Sanicula marilandica

CARROT FAMILY

This erect perennial plant grows up to 1 m tall from thick rootstock, and inhabits moist woods, shady aspen groves, and damp areas near waterways. The basal leaves are long-stalked and palmately divided into five to seven leaflets (usually five). The leaves are generally lance-shaped, with sharply toothed edges. The stem leaves are short-stalked or stalkless. The flowers appear in round clusters and can be yellowish, greenish-white, or white.

The genus name, *Sanicula*, is derived from the Latin *sanare*, which means "to heal," it being believed that the plant had medicinal qualities. The species name is a reference to the State of Maryland, the plant being well distributed in much of the North American continent. The common name, Snakeroot, arises from a practice by Native peoples of using the plant in poultices to treat snakebite. The plant is also known by the common names Black Snakeroot and Maryland Sanicle.

Narrow-Leaved Desert Parsley (Nine-Leaf Biscuit-Root)
Lomatium triternatum

CARROT FAMILY

This perennial herb occurs in dry to moist open sites at foothills to montane elevations, and grows up to 80 cm tall. The leaves are mostly basal, hairy, and divided into segments – often in three sets of three leaflets each. The leaf stalks are irregular in length and clasp the stem. The flowers are very small and yellow, occurring in compound flat-topped clusters (umbels) atop the stems. Often there are a few slender, leafy bracts just below the junction of the individual stalks, but no bracts occur at the base of the flower arrangement.

The origin of the genus name, *Lomatium*, is discussed in the note on Chocolate Tips (*L. dissectum*), shown on page 122. The species name, *triternatum*, means "divided three times in threes," a reference to the leaf construction. Native peoples made extensive use of the plant as food. The Lewis and Clark Expedition journals describe how the Indians ground the roots of the plant into a flour or meal that was then shaped into flat cakes, thus the source for another common name, Nine-Leaf Biscuit-Root. A specimen of the plant was collected by the expedition in present-day Idaho in 1806, and it was later described for science by Frederick Pursh.

Canada Goldenrod
Solidago canadensis

COMPOSITE FAMILY

This is an upright perennial that grows from a creeping rhizome and often forms large colonies in moist soil in meadows, along stream banks, and on lakeshores. The flowering stem is solitary, up to 1 m tall or more, has many branches near the top, and is covered with short, dense hairs. The leaves are all on the stem, of relatively uniform size, and they are lance-shaped to linear, alternate, simple, sharply saw-toothed, and hairy. The flowers are tiny and yellow, occurring in dense, pyramid-shaped clusters at the tops of the stem branches. The branches may curve outward or downward. Each flower has yellow ray and disk florets.

The genus name, *Solidago*, is probably derived from the Latin *solido*, meaning "to make whole or heal," a reference to the supposed healing properties of plants in the genus. The species name indicates the widespread occurrence of the plant in Canada. *Solidago* is a complex and highly variable genus, and a number of the members of the genus bloom in the area. Specific identification can be difficult, and dissection and magnification might be required for absolutely accurate results. That degree of specificity is outside the ambit of this book. Some Native peoples ground the flowers of Goldenrods into a lotion and applied it to bee stings. The once claimed medicinal virtues of the plants are not supported by research results. Goldenrods are also often blamed for causing hay fever in some people, but the pollen in the plants is too heavy to be borne by the wind.

Curly-Cup Gumweed
Grindelia squarrosa

COMPOSITE FAMILY

Virginia Skilton image

This plant is a sticky perennial or biennial that grows up to 1 m tall from a deep taproot, and occurs on roadsides, saline flats, slough margins, riverflats, and dry grasslands. Its leaves are dark green, narrowly oblong, entire or slightly toothed, and glandular-sticky. The lower leaves have long stalks, while the upper ones are stalkless and somewhat clasping, with pointed or rounded tips. The flowers appear as numerous heads, with bright yellow ray florets up to 15 cm long, tapering from the middle to each end. The disk florets are yellow, dense, and up to 2 cm across. The involucral bracts are numerous, sticky, shiny, narrow, overlapping, and sometimes reflexed.

The genus name, *Grindelia*, honours David Grindel, a 19th-century Latvian chemist, pharmacologist, physician and professor of botany at Riga. The species name, *squarrosa*, means "with parts spreading or recurved at the ends," a reference to the reflexed bracts. The common name, Gumweed, alludes to the sticky resins produced by the plant. The plant contains resins, tannic acid, volatile oils, and an alkaloid. Research discloses that it was viewed as a cornucopia of pharmacology by Native peoples and early settlers, being variously used as a contraceptive and to treat poison ivy, bronchitis, asthma, pneumonia, colds, muscle spasms, coughs, liver problems, kidney disease, and syphilis. It was also employed as a veterinary medicine for horses. The plant has a number of locally common names, including Resin Weed, Gum Plant, Tarweed, and Curly-Top Gumweed.

Dandelion
Taraxacum officinale

COMPOSITE FAMILY

This common, introduced plant is found in a variety of habitats the world over, and it is probably the most recognizable flower in our area for most people. The bright yellow flowers have ray florets only, and appear at the top of a smooth stem that arises from a whorl of basal leaves that are lance- to spoon-shaped and deeply incised. The flowers appear from early in the spring until late in the fall, giving this plant undoubtedly the longest blooming time of any flower in our area.

Though everybody seems to recognize this flower, it is interesting to note that more than 1,000 kinds of Dandelions have been described, and specific identification can be difficult. The common name for this plant is thought to be a corruption of the French *dent de lion*, meaning "lion's tooth," a reference to the shape of the leaf. All parts of the plant are edible – the young leaves are eaten raw or cooked as greens, the roots are dried and ground as a coffee substitute, and the flowers can be used to make wine. Some people roll the flower heads in flour and deep-fry them, claiming they have a flavour similar to morel mushrooms when so prepared. The sap from the plant was used in Ireland to treat warts.

Goat's-Beard (Yellow Salsify)
Tragopogon dubius

COMPOSITE FAMILY

A plant of the grasslands, roadsides, ditches, and dry waste areas, Goat's-Beard was introduced from Europe and is also known as Yellow Salsify. The flower is a large solitary, erect yellow head, surrounded by long, narrow, green protruding bracts. The leaves are alternate, fleshy, and narrow, but broad and clasping at the base. The fruit is a mass of white, narrow, ribbed, beaked achenes that resembles the seed pod of a common dandelion but is significantly larger, approaching the size of a softball.

The flowers open on sunny mornings, but then close up around noon and stay closed for the rest of the day. They usually will not open on cloudy or rainy days. The common name, Goat's-Beard, is probably a reference to the mass of white achenes, which is said to resemble a goat's beard. The genus name, *Tragopogon*, is derived from the Greek *tragos*, meaning "he-goat," and *pogon*, meaning "beard." The young leaves and roots from immature plants may be eaten. The leaves and stems exude a milky, latex-like juice when cut, which may be chewed like gum when hardened. A similar species, Purple Salsify or Oyster Plant (*T. porrifolius*) appears in the southern part of the region and on the west coast, but has a purple flower.

Heart-Leaved Arnica
Arnica cordifolia

COMPOSITE FAMILY

Arnica is a common plant of wooded areas in the mountains, foothills and boreal forest. The leaves occur in two to four opposite pairs along the stem, each with long stalks and heart-shaped, serrated blades. The uppermost pair is stalkless and more lance-shaped than the lower leaves. The flowers have 10 to 15 bright yellow ray florets and bright yellow central disk florets.

Without careful dissection of the plant and examination under magnification, recognition of specific members of the genus *Arnica* can be difficult. The leaf structure on an individual plant is often the best clue to species recognition. The genus name, *Arnica*, is derived from the Greek *arnakis*, meaning "lamb's skin," a reference to the woolly bracts and leaf texture on many members of the genus. The species name, *cordifolia*, means "heart-shaped," a reference to the leaves of the plant. A similar species, Mountain Arnica (*A. latifolia*), also known as Broad-Leaved Arnica, inhabits the same habitat. Generally, Mountain Arnica has smaller flowers and round-tipped leaves. Heart-Leaved Arnica occasionally hybridizes with Mountain Arnica, and the resulting plant can be difficult to identify. A number of Native peoples used Arnicas as a poultice for swellings and bruises. Arnicas are said to be poisonous if ingested.

Lyall's Goldenweed (Lyall's Ironplant)
Haplopappus lyallii

COMPOSITE FAMILY

This small perennial grows up to 15 cm tall from a taproot secured in meadows, scree slopes, and gravelly ridges in the alpine zone. The leaves are stemless, lance-shaped and hairy, glandular, and covered in a sticky coating. In addition, the leaves are clumped at the base of the flower stem and extend up the stem. The yellow flower is a solitary composite head with up to 35 ray flowers and yellow disk flowers. The fruits are achenes with brownish bristles.

The genus name, *Haplopappus*, is derived from the Greek *haploos*, which means "simple," and *pappos*, which means "down" or "fluff," a reference to the fruits of the plant. The species name honours David Lyall, a 19th-century Scottish botanist who collected a number of North American plants. This plant might be confused with Golden Fleabane (*Erigeron aureus*), which occurs in the same habitat. However, Golden Fleabane does not have glands to give the leaves the sticky feel that is seen in Lyall's Goldenweed. Golden Fleabane also has mainly basal leaves.

Pineapple Weed (Disc Mayweed)
Matricaria discoidea

COMPOSITE FAMILY

This branching annual grows up to 40 cm tall along roadsides, in ditches, and on disturbed ground. The stem leaves are alternate and fern-like, with finely dissected, narrow segments. Basal leaves have usually fallen off before flowering occurs. The flowers are several to many composite heads, with greenish to yellow disk florets on a cone-shaped or dome-shaped base. There are no ray florets.

The genus name, *Matricaria*, is derived from the Latin *mater* or *matrix*, meaning "mother" or "womb," and *caria*, meaning "dear," and is a reference to use of the plant in the treatment of uterine infections and other gynecological conditions. When crushed, the leaves and flowers of the plant produce a distinctive pineapple aroma, hence the common name. If you tread on the plant without noticing it first, this aroma will quickly become apparent. Some Native peoples used the plant medicinally, while others used it to scent their homes and baby cradles, or as an insect repellent. Meriwether Lewis collected a sample of the plant in 1806 while he was with the Nez Perce Indians in present-day Idaho. The plant is also known as Rayless Chamomile. Wild Chamomile (*M. perforata*) has similar leaves to Pineapple Weed, but its flowers resemble Ox-Eye Daisy (*Leucanthemum vulgare*), shown on page 132. Wild Chamomile has been used by herbalists for treatment of a variety of conditions.

Slender Hawksbeard
Crepis atrabarba

COMPOSITE FAMILY

This taprooted perennial grows up to 70 cm tall at low to middle elevations in dry, open habitats in the region. The basal leaves are very deeply lobed with linear segments. The stem leaves are few, linear, and alternate. The stems are hairy and exude a milky sap when broken. The inflorescence is a flat to round-topped cluster of composite flower heads, each consisting of 10 to 40 bright yellow ray florets, with no disk florets. The involucre (the bracts below the inflorescence) is several rows of greyish, hairy, overlapping bracts which often have black bristles. Each plant will produce a few to 15 yellow flowers. The fruits of the plant are greenish achenes, with a pappus of fine, white, hair-like bristles at the top.

The genus name, *Crepis*, is derived from the Greek *krepis*, meaning "half boot" or "sandal," and it may be a reference to the deeply cut leaves of some members of the genus, which may suggest the thongs of a sandal. The name Hawksbeard was given to the genus *Crepis* by the botanist Asa Gray, and it might refer to the pappus' resemblance to the bristly feathers that surround a hawk's beak. Dwarf Hawksbeard (*C. nana*) is an allied species found in subalpine to alpine zones in the region. It is a low-growing cushion plant that seldom reaches more than 20 cm tall, and has 6 to 12 flowers borne on short stems among the basal leaves. Annual Hawksbeard (*C. tectorum*) is an imported European weed that occurs in the region. It is very similar in appearance to Slender Hawksbeard, but can be taller and usually has fewer flower heads. Its fruits are dark purplish-brown achenes, and the basal leaves usually wither before the plant blooms.

Slender Hawkweed
Hieracium gracile

COMPOSITE FAMILY

This is a plant common to open woods, meadows, roadsides, ditches, and disturbed areas. The yellow flower heads appear in a cluster on ascending stalks. The flowers are composed entirely of ray florets, no disk florets. The leaves are in a basal rosette, broadly lanced to spoon-shaped.

The genus name *Hieracium* is derived from the Greek *hierax*, meaning "hawk," as it was once believed that eating these plants improved a hawk's vision. The species name, *gracile*, means "slender." The leaves, stems, and roots produce a milky latex that was used as a chewing gum by British Columbia tribes. A similar species, Orange Hawkweed (*H. aurantiacum*), shown on page 239, occurs in similar habitat, but is usually found at lower elevations.

Sow Thistle (Perennial Sow Thistle)
Sonchus arvensis

COMPOSITE FAMILY

This is a plant of cultivated fields, roadsides, ditches, and pastures. The flowers have large yellow ray florets similar to dandelion flowers. Sow Thistle is an imported species from Europe. It is not a true thistle. Sow Thistles exude a milky latex when the stem is crushed; true thistles do not.

The common name is derived from the fact that pigs like to eat this plant. The genus name, *Sonchus*, is derived from the Greek word *somphos*, meaning "spongy," a reference to the stems. The species name, *arvensis*, means "of the fields," a reference to the fact that the plant often invades cultivated ground.

Spear-Head Senecio (Arrow-Leaved Groundsel)
Senecio triangularis

COMPOSITE FAMILY

This leafy, lush perennial herb often grows to 1.5 m tall, and occurs in large clumps in moist to wet, open or partly shaded sites, from the foothills to alpine elevations. The leaves are alternate, spearhead- or arrowhead-shaped, squared off at the base, and tapered to the point. The leaves are numerous and well developed along the whole stem of the plant. They are widest near the middle of the stem and are coarsely sharp-toothed. The flowers occur in flat-topped clusters at the top of the plant, and have five to eight bright yellow ray florets surrounding a disk of bright yellow to orange florets.

The genus name, *Senecio*, is derived from the Latin senex, which means "old man." Two opinions emerge as to the intended reference to old man. One says it is because the receptacle to which the flowers are attached is free of hairs, ergo, hairless or bald, like an old man. The other says that the reference is to the grey or white hairs of many members of the genus, ergo, white-haired, like an old man. The species name, *triangularis*, refers to the shape of the leaves, a distinguishing feature of the plant. The common name Ragwort is often applied to members of this genus. It is said to be a reference to the ragged appearance of the leaf margins in many members of the genus. Many members of the genus contain poisonous alkaloids, but livestock seem to find the plants unpalatable. Spear-Head Senecio is often referred to as Giant Ragwort.

Tansy

Tanacetum vulgare

COMPOSITE FAMILY

This plant was introduced from Europe and is common along roadsides, embankments, pastures, fencerows, and disturbed areas. The flowers are yellow and occur in numerous bunches atop multiple stalks. They are flattened and resemble yellow buttons. The leaves are fern-like, dark green, finely dissected, and strong smelling.

Tansies are also known as Button Flowers. The genus name, *Tanacetum*, is derived from the Greek word *athanatos*, meaning "undying" or "immortal," possibly a reference to the long-lasting flowers. In medieval England the plant was placed in shrouds to repel insects and rodents from corpses. It was originally cultivated in North America for its medicinal properties, and it spread from those cultivations. During the Middle Ages a posy of Tansy was thought to ward off the Black Death.

Woolly Groundsel (Woolly Ragwort)
Senecio canus

COMPOSITE FAMILY

This perennial grows from a woody stem base and taproot, with erect stems that are white-woolly and stand up to 40 cm tall. The plant grows in dry areas, from open rocky or sandy places in sagebrush flats to the alpine zone. The whole plant has a silvery appearance, owing to the woolly hairs. The basal leaves and lower stem leaves are elliptic, stalked, and white woolly-hairy. The middle and upper leaves are alternate and become sessile. The rounded inflorescence is composite heads with woolly bases and yellow ray and disk flowers.

The origin of the genus name, *Senecio*, is discussed in the note on Spear-Head Senecio (*S. triangularis*), shown on page 28. The species name, *canus*, is Latin meaning "off-white" or "ashy-coloured," most probably a reference to the white woolly appearance of the plant. The common names Ragwort and Butterweed are often applied to members of this genus.

Yellow Evening-Primrose
Oenothera villosa (also *O. biennis*)

EVENING PRIMROSE FAMILY

An erect, robust, leafy biennial, this plant forms a rosette of leaves the first year, and puts up a tall, leafy stem the second. The flowers have large, bright yellow, cross-shaped stigma, with numerous yellow stamens. The flowers usually open in the evening and fade in the morning, a behaviour adopted because moths are the principal pollinators of the plant.

The plant gets its common name from its habit of blooming at dusk. The genus name, *Oenothera*, is derived from the Greek word meaning "wine scented" – *oinos* meaning "wine," and *thera* meaning "to induce wine drinking." The name is said to arise because an allied European plant was thought to induce a taste for wine. The roots of the first-year plant were often dug and boiled for food, or were dried for later use. They are said to be nutritious and have a nut-like flavour. Seed oil from the plant is used for medicinal purposes. Another member of the genus, Pale Evening-Primrose (*O. pallida*) is found in the region in dry, sandy habitat. It has white (sometimes pinkish) flowers and white, shredding stems.

Bracted Lousewort (Wood Betony)
Pedicularis bracteosa

FIGWORT FAMILY

Gill Ross image

This plant can grow to a height of up to 1 m, and is found in subalpine and alpine elevations in moist forests, meadows, and clearings. The leaves are similar to those of ferns – divided into long, narrow, toothed segments – and are attached to the upper portions of the stem of the plant. The flowers vary from yellow to red to purple. The flowers arise from the axils of leafy bracts, and occur in an elongated cluster at the top of the stem. The flowers have a two-lipped corolla, with the upper lip arched downward and the lower lip curving upward, giving the impression of a bird's beak.

The genus name, *Pedicularis*, is from the Latin *pedis*, "louse," and *pediculosus*, "lousy," and plants of this genus are generally referred to as Louseworts. There apparently was a belief at one time that cattle that ate Louseworts were more likely to be afflicted by lice. The species name, *bracteosa*, refers to the leafy bracts below each flower. Louseworts are partially parasitic on the roots of other plants, and derive some of their nutrients from adjacent plants. Herbalists favour the plant as a sedative. The common name Betony is said to derive from an old Iberian word that meant "to cure all ills." The plant is also known by the locally common name Fernleaf.

Butter and Eggs (Toadflax)
Linaria vulgaris

FIGWORT FAMILY

This is a common plant of roadsides, ditches, fields, and disturbed areas that grows up to 1 m tall. It is also known as Toadflax. The leaves are alternate, dark green, and narrow. The flowers are similar in shape to Snapdragons. The bright yellow flowers with orange throats occur in dense, terminal clusters at the tops of erect stems. The corolla is spurred at the base and two-lipped; the upper lip two-lobed, the lower one three-lobed.

The flower takes one of its common names from the yellow and orange tones that resemble the colours of butter and eggs. As to the origin of the other common name, Toadflax, there are two schools of thought. In early English, "toad" meant "false" or "useless," ergo "useless flax" or "false flax" – the leaves of this plant resembling those of Flax. The other school of thought attributes the name "toad" to the resemblance of the flower to that of a toad's mouth. Toadflax was introduced to North America from Europe as a garden plant, but escapees from the garden have become noxious weeds. The plant was used in early Europe to treat jaundice, piles, and eye infections, and was also boiled in milk to make a fly poison. The genus name, *Linaria*, refers to the general similarity of the leaves of this plant to those of Flax. Dalmatian Toadflax (*L. dalmatica*) is a similar species that appears in the same habitat. It has clasping, broadly oval leaves, and larger flowers.

Common Mullein
Verbascum thapsis

FIGWORT FAMILY

A Eurasian import that grows up to 2 m tall, Mullein is quite common along roadsides, gravelly places, and dry slopes. The plant is a biennial, taking two years to produce flowers. In the first year, the plant puts out a rosette of large leaves which are very soft to the touch, much like velvet or flannel. From those leaves surges the strong, sentinel-like stalk in the second year. The small yellow flowers appear randomly from a flowering spike atop the stalk. It appears that at no time do all the flowers bloom together. After flowering, the dead stalk turns dark brown and may persist for many months.

The genus name, *Verbascum*, is a corrupted form of *Barbascum*, the ancient Latin name for the plant. A common name for the plant is Flannel Mullein, a reference to the soft texture of the basal leaves. Mullein is derived from the Latin *mollis*, which means "soft." The dried leaves of the plant were sometimes smoked by Native peoples, and the plant is sometimes called Indian Tobacco. The crushed leaves were often used as a poultice applied to swelling and wounds because the chemicals in the plant soothe irritated tissues and act as a sedative.

Yellow Monkeyflower
Mimulus guttatus

FIGWORT FAMILY

This plant occurs, often in large patches, along streams, seeps, and in moist meadows from low to high elevations. The plant is quite variable, but always spectacular when found. The bright yellow flowers resemble Snapdragons, and occur in clusters. The flowers are two-lipped, trumpet-shaped, and hairy in the throat. The flowers usually have red or purple dots on the lower lip, giving the appearance of a grinning face.

The genus name, *Mimulus*, is derived from the Latin *mimus*, meaning "mimic" or "actor," a reference to the "face" seen on the flower. The species name, *guttatus*, means "spotted" or "speckled." The plant is also known by the locally common name Seep Monkeyflower. A related species, Red Monkeyflower, (*M. lewisii*), shown on page 248, also occurs in the region.

Yellow Penstemon (Yellow Beardtongue)
Penstemon confertus

FIGWORT FAMILY

This is a plant of moist to dry meadows, woodlands, stream banks, hillsides and mountains, and occurs from the prairie to the alpine zone. The small pale yellow flowers are numerous, and appear in whorled, interrupted clusters along the upper part of the stem. Each flower is tube-shaped, and has two lips. The lower lip is three-lobed and bearded at the throat; the upper lip is two-lobed.

The origin of the common name, Beardtongue, and the genus name, Penstemon, is explained in the narrative on Small-Flowered Penstemon (*P. procerus*), shown on page 84. The species name, *confertus*, is Latin, meaning "crowded," a reference to the numerous flowers in the clusters. A number of Penstemons appear in the region.

Yellow Rattle
Rhinanthus minor

FIGWORT FAMILY

Virginia Skilton image

This plant has erect single or partially branched flowering stems that can stand up to 50 cm tall, and is found in low to subalpine elevations on dry plateaus, moist clearings, meadows, and disturbed areas. The leaves are lance-shaped with toothed margins, opposite, and have short stems. The flowers are yellow, and appear in a terminal cluster. Each flower has a two-lipped corolla protruding from an encasing, flattened, inflated calyx. The upper lip of the flower is two-lobed and forms a hood; the lower lip is three-lobed.

The genus name, *Rhinanthus*, is derived from the Greek *rhinos*, which means "nose" or "snout," and *anthos*, meaning "flower," a reference to the shape of the flower. Yellow Rattle is a partially parasitic plant that attaches itself to the roots of adjacent plants to obtain water and nutrients. The common name arises because the mature fruit capsules make a rattling noise when shaken. The plant has several other names that might be locally common, including Money-Grass, Rattlebag, Rattlebox, and Shepherd's-Coffin.

Golden Corydalis
Corydalis aurea

FUMITORY FAMILY

This plant of open woods, roadsides, disturbed places, and stream banks, is an erect or spreading, branched, leafy biennial or annual. It germinates in the fall and overwinters as a seedling. In the spring, it grows rapidly, flowers, and then dies. The yellow flowers are irregularly shaped, rather like the flowers of the Pea Family, with keels at the tips. A long, nectar-producing spur extends backward from the upper petal.

The genus name, *Corydalis*, is derived from the Greek *korydallis*, meaning "crested lark," a reference to the spur of the petal resembling the spur of a lark. The species name, *aurea*, means "golden." Corydalis is generally considered poisonous because it contains isoquinoline and other alkaloids. Some poisoning of livestock has been reported. A similar species, Pink Corydalis (*C. sempervirens*), appears in similar habitat in the region, but it has pink flowers with yellow tips, and is a taller and more erect plant.

Black Twinberry (Bracted Honeysuckle)
Lonicera involucrata

HONEYSUCKLE FAMILY

This plant is a shrub that grows up to 2 m tall in moist woods and along stream banks. The flowers are yellow and occur in pairs, arising from the axils of the leaves. The flowers are overlain by a purple to reddish leafy bract. As the fruit ripens, the bract remains, enlarges, and darkens in colour. The ripe fruits occur in pairs and are black.

The genus name, *Lonicera*, honours the 16th-century German herbalist, physician, and botanist Adam Lonitzer. The species name, *involucrata*, is from the Latin *involucrum*, meaning "wrapper" or "case," and refers to the prominent bracts. Some Native peoples believed that the Black Twinberries were poisonous, and would make one crazy. They are bitter to the taste, but serve as food for a variety of birds and small mammals. The plant is also known by the locally common name of Bracted Honeysuckle.

Glacier Lily (Yellow Avalanche Lily)
Erythronium grandiflorum

LILY FAMILY

This gorgeous lily is one of the first blooms in the spring, often appearing at the edges of receding snowbanks on mountain slopes, thus the common names. The bright yellow flowers appear at the top of a leafless stem, usually solitary, though a plant might have up to three flowers. The flowers are nodding, with six tepals that are tapered to the tip and reflexed, with white, yellow or brown anthers. The leaves, usually two, are attached near the base of the stem and are broadly oblong, glossy, and unmarked.

The genus name, *Erythronium,* is derived from the Greek *erythrus,* meaning "red," a reference to a similar Old World species (*E. dens-canis*), which has pink to reddish flowers and was said to produce a red dye. The species name, *grandiflorum,* means "large flowered." Glacier Lilies are a favoured food of bears. Bears have been observed digging up the yellow flowers and bulbs, then leaving them to wilt on the ground, returning days later to eat them. Evidently the bears are aware that the bulbs have an increased sweetness after being exposed to the air. Some Native peoples gathered the bulbs as food. The bulbs are inedible when raw, but prolonged steaming converts the indigestible carbohydrates into edible fructose. Drying the bulbs also helps in this process. Glacier Lilies often appear in large numbers, turning the hillsides yellow with their profusion. Two other common local names for the plant are Slide Lily and Dog's Tooth Violet.

Yellowbell
Fritillaria pudica

LILY FAMILY

This diminutive flower is a harbinger of spring, blooming often just after snowmelt in dry grasslands and dry open Ponderosa pine forests. It can easily be overlooked because of its small size, usually standing only about 15 cm tall. The yellow, drooping, bell-shaped flowers are very distinctive. The flowers turn orange to brick-red as they age. The leaves (usually two or three) are linear to lance-shaped, and appear more or less opposite about halfway up the stem. The Yellowbell sometimes appears with two flowers on a stem, but single blooms are more common.

The origin of the genus name, *Fritillaria*, is discussed in the note on Chocolate Lily (*F. affinis*), shown on page 90. The species name, *pudica*, means "bashful," and is probably a reference to the nodding attitude of the flower on the stem. Native peoples gathered the bulbs and used them as food, eating them both raw and cooked.

Douglas Maple (Rocky Mountain Maple)
Acer glabrum

MAPLE FAMILY

This deciduous shrub or small tree is found in moist, sheltered sites from foothills to subalpine zones. The plant has graceful, wide-spreading branches. The young twigs are smooth and cherry-red, turning grey with age. The leaves are opposite and typical of maples – three-lobed, with an unequal and sharply toothed margin. The yellowish-green flowers are short-lived and fragrant, with five petals and five sepals, hanging in loose clusters. The fruits are V-shaped pairs of winged seeds, joined at the point of attachment to the shrub. The fruit is known as a "samara."

Acer is Latin for "maple." The species name, *glabrum*, means "smooth, without hair." Native peoples had a variety of uses for this plant, including the manufacture of cordage, cradle frames, tepee pegs and joiners, bows, snowshoes, drum hoops, and fish traps.

Golden Draba (Golden Whitlow Grass)
Draba aurea

MUSTARD FAMILY

This member of the Mustard Family grows up to 50 cm tall, and occurs on rocky slopes, in open woods, and in meadows from the montane to the alpine zones. The basal leaves are lance-shaped, hairy, and appear in a rosette. The stem leaves are stalkless, alternate, somewhat clasping on the stem, lance-shaped, hairy, and distributed up the stem. The flowers are four-petalled, bright yellow, and appear in a cluster at the top of the stem. Mustards typically have four petals in a cruciform shape. At one time, the Mustard Family was known as Cruciferae, from the Latin *crux/crucis*, which means "cross."

The genus name, *Draba*, is derived from the Greek *drabe*, which means "acrid," a reference to the sap of some members of the Mustard Family. The species name, *aurea*, means "golden," a reference to the flower colour. Draba has traditionally been used to treat whitlow, a painful infection of the fingers that is caused by the *herpes simplex* virus, hence the common name, Yellow Whitlow Grass. A number of Drabas appear in the region, and they can be difficult to differentiate from one another without serious magnification. Payson's Draba (*D. paysonii*), is a low-growing matted plant, with numerous clusters of yellow flowers. White Draba (*D. lonchocarpa*), also known as White Whitlow Grass, is also an alpine matting plant and has white flowers.

43

Prairie Rocket
Erysimum asperum

MUSTARD FAMILY

This erect, robust plant grows up to 50 cm tall or more in dry, sandy grasslands, particularly in the southeastern parts of the region. The bright yellow flowers grow at the terminal ends of stout branching stems, and appear in rounded clusters. The stem leaves on the plant are simple, alternate, and lance-shaped.

The genus name, *Erysimum*, is derived from the Greek *erysis*, meaning "to draw out," a reference to the acrid juices of such plants being used in poultices. The species name, *asperum*, is Latin meaning "rough," likely a reference to the stiff hairs found on the plant. At one time, children were treated for worms with a concoction made up of the crushed seeds of this plant mixed in water.

Soopolallie (Canadian Buffaloberry)
Shepherdia canadensis

OLEASTER FAMILY

This deciduous shrub grows up to 3 m tall, and is often the dominant understorey cover in lodgepole pine forests. All parts of the plant are covered with rust-coloured, shiny scales, giving the whole plant an orange, rusty appearance. The leaves are leathery and thick, green and glossy on the upper surface, while the lower surface is covered with white hairs and sprinkled with rusty coloured dots. The plant is dioecious, that is, the male and female flowers appear on separate plants. The small, inconspicuous yellow flowers often appear on the branches of the plant prior to the arrival of the leaves. The male flowers have four stamens, while the female flowers have none. In the fall, the female shrubs will be covered with small, translucent berries that are predominantly red.

The genus name, *Shepherdia*, is to honour the 18th-century English botanist John Shepherd. The common name, Soopolallie, is from the Chinook tribe – soop meaning "soap," and olallie, meaning "berry" – a reference to the fact that when beaten in water the red berries produce a pink, soapy froth that some Native peoples liked to drink. The foam is derived from the bitter chemical saponins contained in the berries. Bears seem to relish the berries, and early settlers reported that buffalo browsed them, thus two of the common names. Other common names for the plant include Soapberry, Russet Buffaloberry, and Bearberry.

Wolf Willow (Silverberry)
Elaeagnus commutata

OLEASTER FAMILY

This deciduous shrub grows up to 4 m tall, and often occurs in dense stands. The twigs are densely covered with rusty brown scales, and the leaves are alternate, oval, silvery in colour, and covered with small scales. The flowers are funnel-shaped, and have four yellow lobes, occurring at the leaf axils. The flowers are very fragrant with a distinctive aroma. The fruits are silvery, round to egg-shaped berries and usually persist throughout the winter.

The genus name, *Elaeagnus*, is derived from the Greek *elaia*, meaning "olive," and *agnos*, meaning "willow." Native peoples used the tough, fibrous bark of the plant to make bags, baskets, and rope. The berries of the plant were often used as beads for personal adornment. A very similar plant, Russian Olive (*E. angustifolia*), was introduced from Europe and used as a windbreak, but it is a larger plant and has thorns.

Yellow Lady's Slipper
Cypripedium parviflorum (formerly *C. calceolus*)

ORCHID FAMILY

This is an orchid of bogs, damp woods, and stream banks. The leaves are alternate, with two to four per stem, broadly elliptic, and clasping. The yellow flowers usually occur one per stem, and resemble a small shoe. The sepals and lateral petals are similar, greenish-yellow to brownish, with twisted, wavy margins. The lower petal forms a prominent pouch-shaped yellow lip with purple dotting around the puckered opening.

The origin of the genus name, *Cypripedium*, is discussed in the note for Mountain Lady's Slipper (*C. montanum*), shown on page 183. Yellow Lady's Slipper was originally known as *Calceolus mariae*, which translates into "St. Mary's little shoe." Bees enter the opening of the "slipper" and cannot exit without being covered in pollen. This lovely flower has suffered large range reductions as a result of picking and attempted transplantation, which almost always fails.

Field Locoweed
Oxytropis campestris

PEA FAMILY

This early-blooming plant is widespread and common in rocky outcrops, roadsides, and dry open woods in the region. The leaves are mainly basal, with elliptical leaflets and dense hairs. The pale yellow, pea-like flowers bloom in clusters at the top of a leafless, hairy stem.

The genus name, *Oxytropis,* is derived from the Greek *oxys,* meaning "sharp" or "bitter," and *tropis,* meaning "keel," a reference to the sharp keel on the flower. The species name, *campestris,* is Latin meaning "field loving." Field Locoweed is also known by the locally common name Columbia River Locoweed. The plant is poisonous to cattle, sheep, and horses, owing to its high content of alkaloids that cause blind staggers. This loss of muscle control in animals that have ingested the plant is the origin of the common name for the flower, loco being Spanish for "mad" or "foolish." Plants of this genus might be confused with those of *Astragalus,* the Milk-Vetches, in which the flowers are similar. However, the flowers of Locoweeds are usually on leafless stalks and always have a pointed projection at the tip of the keel.

Sulphur Lupine
Lupinus sulphureus

PEA FAMILY

Virginia Skilton image

This plant is a slender, erect, mostly unbranched plant that is stiff-hairy and grows up to 80 cm tall in grasslands and dry open Ponderosa forests at low to middle elevations. The leaves are alternate, mostly on the stem, palmately compound, with 8 to 13 leaflets, and sharp-pointed. The stalks on the stem leaves are roughly the same length as the leaflets. The few basal leaves have longer stalks and are hairy on both surfaces. The yellow (sometimes white) pea-like flowers are hairy and whorled or scattered in a raceme along the upper part of the stem.

The origin of the genus name, *Lupinus*, is discussed in the note on Silky Lupine (*L. sericia*), shown on page 98. The species name, *sulphureus*, refers to the colour of the flowers. Lupines have distinctive leaves, but specific identification can be difficult in this highly variable plant. Hybridization also can complicate specific identification. This species will hybridize with Silky Lupine where their range overlaps. The fruits of Lupine contain an alkaloid and may be poisonous to some livestock, particularly sheep.

Yellow Hedysarum
Hedysarum sulphurescens

PEA FAMILY

This is a plant of stream banks, grasslands, open forests, and clearings. The flowers are pea-like, yellowish to nearly white, drooping, and appear usually along one side of the stem in elongated clusters (racemes). The fruits of the plant are long, flattened, pendulous pods, with conspicuous winged edges and constrictions between each of the seeds.

The genus name, *Hedysarum*, is derived from the Greek *hedys*, meaning "sweet," and *aroma*, meaning "smell." Yellow Hedysarum is also called Yellow Sweet Vetch. It is an extremely important food for grizzly bears, which eat the roots in the spring and fall. Northern Sweet-Vetch (*H. boreale*) is a related species that occurs in the region. It has fragrant purple flowers.

Large-Flowered Collomia
Collomia grandiflora

PHLOX FAMILY

Werner Eigelsreiter image

This robust annual occurs in dry open woods and on grassy slopes from valley to middle elevations. The flowering stem may be solitary or branched, and stands up to 1 m tall. The leaves are narrow, alternate on the stem, lance-shaped, and smooth on the margins (entire). The stem supports a closely packed head of white to pale yellow to salmon-coloured trumpet-shaped flowers about 3 cm long. The floral tube has five gently pointed lobes. There are leafy bracts just below the flower head. The flowers bloom early and last a long time.

The genus name, Collomia, is derived from the Greek *kolla*, which means "glue," a reference to a sticky secretion around the seeds, particularly when they are moistened. The species name refers to the relatively large flowering head. Narrow-Leaved Collomia (*C. linearis*) is an allied species that blooms in similar habitat in the region. It is a shorter plant, standing only 60 cm tall, and it has pink to bluish to white flowers that occur in a cluster at the stem top.

Fringed Loosestrife
Lysimachia ciliata

PRIMROSE FAMILY

Anne Elliott image

This is an erect plant, growing up to 1 m tall, that occurs in prairie to montane zones in woods, damp meadows, thickets, and on stream banks. The leaves are large, opposite, prominently veined, oval to broadly lance-shaped, rounded at the base, pointed at the end, and fringed with white hairs. The large yellow flowers appear from the upper leaf axils, and have five petals with fringed margins and reddish glandular bases. The tips of the petals are usually unevenly pointed.

The genus name, *Lysimachia*, is derived from the Greek *lysis*, which means "to release" or "loosening," and *mache*, which means "strife" or "battle." The exact taxonomic reference to this plant is unclear, but two stories are presented by the authorities as to the connection. The first holds that Pliny, a Roman historian, reported that Lysimachos, King of Thrace and companion of Alexander the Great, used the plant to calm an angry bull. The other story, similar in part, holds that Loosestrife deters flies and gnats, and was attached to the harnesses of draught animals to quiet them. Interestingly, it is also said that the plant was burned inside houses to repel snakes and insects.

Bitterbrush (Antelope Brush)
Purshia tridentata

ROSE FAMILY

This deciduous shrub grows up to 2 m tall in dry sites in the plains and foothills of the region. The plant is rigidly branched, and the branches are covered with dense woolly hairs. The flowers are numerous, funnel-shaped and bright yellow, appearing from the branches of the shrub, usually in the spring.

Antelope Brush is important browse for deer and elk, and the seeds from the plant are favourites of small burrowing mammals such as chipmunks, ground squirrels, and mice. The plants resemble sagebrush but actually are a member of the Rose Family. The plant was first described for science by Frederick Pursh from a specimen collected in present-day Montana by Meriwether Lewis of the Lewis and Clark Expedition. Pursh originally named the plant *Tigarea tridentalis*, but later botanists created a new genus and named it in honour of Pursh. The plant is also known by the locally common name Pursh's Bitterbrush.

Drummond's Mountain Avens (Yellow Mountain Avens)
Dryas drummondii

ROSE FAMILY

This is a plant of gravelly streams and river banks, slopes and roadsides in the foothills and mountains. The yellow flower is solitary and nodding, with black, glandular hairs, blooming on the top of a hairy, leafless stalk. Leaves are alternate, leathery and wrinkly, dark green above and whitish-hairy beneath. The leaves are rounded at the tip, but wedge-shaped at the base. The margins are scalloped and slightly rolled under. The fruit consists of many achenes, each with a silky, golden yellow, feathery plume that becomes twisted around the others into a tight spiral that later opens into a fluffy mass, dispersing the seeds on the wind.

The genus name, *Dryas,* was named for the Dryades, the wood nymphs of Greek mythology. The species name, *drummondii,* honours Thomas Drummond, a Scottish naturalist who accompanied Franklin on his expedition to find the Northwest Passage. Some Native peoples used the plant for medicinal purposes, it being thought that it had healing properties for heart, kidney, and bladder trouble. This small flower likes calcium-rich soil, gravelly streams, and riverbanks, often creating large colonies of flowers. A related species, White Dryad (*D. octopetala*) is shown on page 207.

Large-Leaved Avens
Geum macrophyllum

ROSE FAMILY

This is an erect, hairy, tall perennial that grows in moist woods, along rivers and streams and in thickets from low to subalpine elevations. The flowers are bright yellow and saucer-shaped, with five petals. The flowers usually appear at the tip of a tall, slender stem. The basal leaves of the plant occur in a cluster and are pinnately compound, deeply lobed, and toothed. The terminal leaf is rounded, shallowly lobed and much larger than the lateral leaves below it on the stem. The fruits are achenes that have hooks on them, and they will cling to the clothing of passersby and the fur of animals as a seed dispersal mechanism.

The genus name, *Geum*, is from the Greek *geyo*, meaning "to stimulate," as the shredded roots of a related Mediterranean species were used. The species name, *macrophyllum*, is a reference to the large terminal leaf of the plant. Native peoples made extensive use of the plant in medicinal concoctions. Leaves and roots of the plant were used in poultices applied to cuts, bruises and boils. A tea made from the plant was used both to prevent conception and to soothe the womb after childbirth.

Shrubby Cinquefoil
Potentilla fruticosa

ROSE FAMILY

This low deciduous shrub is found in dry meadows, on rocky slopes, and in gravelly river courses at low to subalpine elevations. The leaves are alternate, divided into three to seven (usually five) leaflets that are lightly hairy, greyish-green, and often have curled edges. The flowers are golden yellow and saucer-shaped, with five rounded petals, usually blooming as a solitary at the end of branches. The flowers are often smaller and paler at lower elevations; larger and brighter at higher elevations.

The origin of the genus name, *Potentilla*, is explained in the note on Silver-weed (*P. anserina*), shown on page 58. The species name, *fruticosa*, means "shrubby," and refers to the plant forming a low, rounded bush, usually about 1 m tall. The common name is from the Latin *quinque*, meaning "five," and *folium*, meaning "leaf," a reference to the fact that many Potentilla species have five leaflets and the flower parts are in fives. Shrubby Cinquefoil is a popular garden ornamental, and is easily propagated from cuttings.

Sibbaldia
Sibbaldia procumbens

ROSE FAMILY

Virginia Skilton image

This is a ground-hugging perennial that forms cushions in the alpine zone. The prostrate stems branch from the base, and terminate in clusters of three leaflets, similar to clover. These leaflets, however, are wedge-shaped, and each has three prominent teeth at the blunt end. White hairs cover both surfaces of the leaflets. The pale yellow flowers are generally saucer-shaped and appear in clusters at the tops of the flowering stems. Each flower is made up of five yellow petals that alternate with five hairy, green sepals. The petals are about half as long as the sepals.

The genus name, *Sibbaldia*, honours Sir Robert Sibbald, an 18th-century Scottish physician and botanist. The species name, *procumbens*, means "prone" or "flat on the ground," a reference to the growth habit of the plant. Some confusion might arise if one encounters Sibbaldia in the same area as some member of the Cinquefoils (*Potentilla* spp). If the plant has three distinct teeth only at the end of the leaflets, it is Sibbaldia.

Silverweed
Potentilla anserina

ROSE FAMILY

This plant is a low, prostrate perennial that grows from thick rootstock and reddish-coloured runners in moist meadows and on riverbanks, lakeshores, and slough margins. The leaves are basal, compound, toothed, and pinnate, with 7 to 25 leaflets per leaf. Each leaflet is silky-haired and green to silvery on top, lighter underneath. The flowers are bright yellow and solitary on leafless stems, with rounded petals in fives. The sepals are light green and hairy, and appear between the petals.

The common name is derived from the silvery colour of the leaves. The genus name, *Potentilla*, is derived from the Latin *potens*, which means "powerful," an allusion to the supposed medicinal properties of plants of this genus. The species name, *anserina*, means "of or pertaining to geese," and has been variously explained as an allusion to the soft, hairy leaves of the plant being like down, or, alternatively, to the fact that geese might eat the plant in its native habitat. Native peoples used the roots of the plant as food, eating it either raw or cooked. Native peoples also extracted a red dye from the plant and used the runners as cordage material.

Sticky Cinquefoil
Potentilla glandulosa

ROSE FAMILY

This plant inhabits open forests and meadows at low to middle elevations. It grows to about 40 cm tall from a branched rootstock, and the leaves and stems are covered with glandular hairs that exude a sticky, aromatic fluid. The leaves are mainly basal and pinnately divided into five to nine sharply toothed oval leaflets. The flowers are typical of the Potentillas and are pale yellow to creamy white, occurring in small open clusters at the top of the stems.

The origin of the genus name, Potentilla, is explained in the note on Silverweed (*P. anserina*), shown on page 58. The species name, *glandulosa*, is a reference to the glandular hairs that cover the plant. This plant, like other members of the family, has high tannin content and is used as an astringent and anti-inflammatory. Sulphur Cinquefoil (*P. recta*), is a related species that occurs in similar habitat. It is an invasive weed introduced from Eurasia. It grows up to 80 cm tall and has mostly stem leaves that are palmately divided into five to seven deeply toothed leaflets, with pale yellow flowers that are in a flat-topped cluster at the top of the stem.

Yellow Mountain Saxifrage
Saxifraga aizoides

SAXIFRAGE FAMILY

This is a ground-hugging sturdy perennial that forms loose mats or cushions on moist sand, gravel, stream banks, and stones in the alpine zone. The upright stems are up to 10 cm tall, and are crowded with fat, succulent, linear leaves that have an abrupt tip. The leaves are covered in very small, pale hairs. The flowers appear at the tops of the stems, pale yellow, often spotted with orange. The flowers have five petals, which may be ragged at the tips. There are ten stamens with conspicuously large anthers.

The origin of the genus name, *Saxifraga*, is explained in the note on Alaska Saxifrage (*S. ferruginea*), shown on page 210. The species name, *aizoides*, is Greek, derived from *aei*, meaning "always," and *zoon*, meaning "alive," a reference to the ability of this plant to survive in the bleak environment it inhabits.

Western St. John's Wort
Hypericum scouleri (also *H. formosum*)

ST. JOHN'S WORT FAMILY

Gill Ross image

This perennial appears in moist places from foothills to the alpine zone and grows to 25 cm tall. The leaves are opposite, egg-shaped to elliptical, 1–3 cm long, somewhat clasping at the base, and usually have purplish-black dots along the edges. The bright yellow flowers have five petals and occur in open clusters at the top of the plant. The stamens are numerous and often look like a starburst.

The common name applied to members of this genus refers to St. John the Baptist. The spots on the leaves were said to ooze blood on the day of his execution. The genus name, *Hypericum*, is the Greek name for a European member of the genus. The species name, *scouleri*, honours John Scouler, a 19th-century Scottish physician and naturalist who collected plant specimens in western North America and the Galapagos Islands. A related species, Common St. John's Wort (*H. perforatum*), is a noxious European weed that has been introduced into North America and has spread across the continent at lower elevations. Its flowers resemble those of this species. Plants in the genus contain compounds that are thought to be potent antiviral agents, and the genus is being studied by AIDS researchers.

Lance-Leaved Stonecrop
Sedum lanceolatum

STONECROP FAMILY

This fleshy perennial with reddish stems grows up to 15 cm tall on dry, rocky, open slopes and in meadows and rock crevices from low elevations to above timberline. The leaves are numerous, round in cross-section, alternate, fleshy, overlapping and mostly basal. The flowers are bright yellow, star-shaped with sharply pointed petals, and occur in dense, flat-topped clusters atop short stems.

The genus name, *Sedum*, is derived from the Latin *sedere*, which means "to sit," a reference to the plant's low-growing habit. The species name, *lanceolatum*, refers to the plant's lance-shaped leaves. The common name Stonecrop refers to the plant's normal habitat. Some authorities say the plant is edible, while others disagree. Roseroot (*S. rosea*), shown on page 285, is a related species that occurs in subalpine to alpine habitats and has red flowers. Broad-Leaved Stonecrop (*S. spathulifolium*), is also a related species that occurs in the region. It has similar flowers to Lance-Leaved Stonecrop, but its leaves are spoon-shaped and fleshy, and it occurs generally at lower elevations.

Round-Leaved Violet
Viola orbiculata

VIOLET FAMILY

This diminutive flower is an early bloomer, appearing right behind the melting snows in moist coniferous forests. The leaves lie flat on the ground and are oval to nearly circular, often remaining green through the winter. The flowers are lemon yellow and have purplish pencil marking on the lower three petals. The markings direct insects to the source of the nectar.

The origin of the genus name, *Viola*, is discussed in the note on Early Blue Violet (*V. adunca*), shown on page 104. The species name, *orbiculata*, is a reference to the shape of the leaves. Candied flowers of this plant are often used for decorating cakes and pastries.

Yellow Wood Violet (Stream Violet)
Viola glabella

VIOLET FAMILY

This beautiful yellow violet occurs in moist woods, and often is found in extensive patches. There are smooth, heart-shaped, serrate leaves on the upper part of the plant stem. The flowers have very short spurs, and the interior of the side petals often exhibit a white beard.

The origin of the genus name, *Viola*, is discussed in the note on Early Blue Violet (*V. adunca*), shown on page 104. The species name, *glabella*, is Latin meaning "smooth-skinned," a reference to the smooth leaves. The flower is also commonly referred to as Smooth Violet and Stream Violet.

Yellow Pond Lily (Yellow Water Lily)
Nuphar variegatum

WATER LILY FAMILY

This plant of ponds, lakes, and slow-moving streams is perhaps the most recognizable water plant in the area. This aquatic perennial grows from a thick rootstock, producing cord-like stems. The floating leaves are borne singly on long stems, are up to 15 cm long, waxy on the surface, round and broadly oval, and heart-shaped at the base. The large flowers protrude from the water's surface and are solitary on long stalks, with six sepals that are showy, greenish-yellow on the outside and tinged with red on the inside. Numerous yellow stamens surround a large pistil.

The origin of the genus name, *Nuphar,* is the matter of some dispute among the authorities. Some say it comes from the Persian word *nenuphar,* some say it comes from the Arabic word *naufar.* All agree that both words mean "pond lily." The species name, *variegatum,* is Latin meaning "with patches of different colours," a reference to the colours in the sepals. A number of Native peoples employed the plant as food, eating it raw, boiled, baked or ground into flour. Some Native peoples used the plant medicinally to treat venereal disease, make poultices or treat horses. The plant provides cover for fish and food for waterfowl and water mammals.

Blue and Purple Flowers

This section includes flowers that are predominantly blue or purple when encountered in the field – ranging from pale blue to deep purple, light violet to lavender. Some of the lighter colours of blue and purple might shade into pinks, so if you do not find the flower your are looking for here, check the other sections of this book.

Common Butterwort
Pinguicula vulgaris

BLADDERWORT FAMILY

This small plant is one of only a few carnivorous plants in the area. It grows from fibrous roots in bogs, seeps, wetlands, stream banks, and lakeshores, from valleys to the subalpine zone. The pale green to yellowish leaves are basal, short-stalked, somewhat overlapping, curled in at the margins, and form a rosette on the ground. The leaves have glandular hairs on their upper surface that exude a sticky substance which attracts and ensnares small insects. The insects are then digested by the plant, enabling it to obtain nitrogen and other nutrients. The flower is pale to dark purple, solitary, and occurs atop a leafless stem.

The common name, Butterwort, is said to come from the buttery feel of the leaves, *wort* being an Old English word that means "herb" or "a plant." The genus name, *Pinguicula*, is the diminutive of the Latin word *pinguis*, which means "fat," also a reference to the soft, greasy-feeling leaves of the plant.

Alpine Forget-Me-Not
Myosotis alpestris

BORAGE FAMILY

This beautiful, fragrant little flower is easily recognized by its wheel-shaped blue corolla and its prominent yellow eye. This plant occurs, often in clumps, in moist subalpine and alpine meadows. The leaves are lance-shaped to linear. The lower leaves have short stems, but the upper ones are clasping. The stems are covered with long, soft hairs.

The genus name, *Myosotis*, is derived from the Greek *mus*, meaning "mouse," and *ous*, meaning "ear," descriptive of the furred leaves of some members of the genus. There seems to be some dispute as to the origin of the common name. One school of thought holds that the name dates back to the 1500s when tradition held that a blue flower was worn to retain a lover's affections. Another school of thought holds that a couple was walking along the Danube River and the woman remarked on the beauty of some blue flowers blooming on a steep slope by the river. The man attempted to fetch the flowers for his sweetheart, but fell into the river, asking her as he fell to "forget me not." Alpine Forget-Me-Not is the State flower of Alaska.

Blueweed (Viper's Bugloss)
Echium vulgare

BORAGE FAMILY

This European import grows up to 80 cm tall and is found on roadsides and in pastures and disturbed areas throughout Canada. It was first introduced as a garden ornamental, but it escaped and is now a problem weed, forcing out native vegetation. The flowers are distributed up a stout central stalk that is hairy in appearance. The flowers are a spectacular bright blue, funnel-shaped, with unequal lobes. The fruits are rough nutlets that are said to resemble a viper's head.

The genus name, *Echium*, is derived from the Greek *echis*, meaning "viper," most probably a reference to the shape of the seed of the plant. At one time the plant was believed to be useful in treating snakebite. The common name, Bugloss, is derived from the Greek *bous*, meaning "ox," and *glossa*, meaning "tongue," the reference being that the rough leaves of this plant resemble the tongue of an ox. The bristly hairs on the leaves and stem of the plant cause severe skin irritation in many people. Infestations of this noxious weed are only too common in many parts of Canada, giving rise to another locally common name, Blue Devil.

Stickseed
Hackelia floribunda

BORAGE FAMILY

This plant is a hairy biennial or short-lived perennial that has stiffly erect stems and grows to 1 m tall. The small, yellow-centred, blue flowers occur in loose clusters on curving stalks near the top of the plant. The fruits are nutlets that are keeled in the middle and attached to a pyramid-shaped base. Each nutlet has rows of barbed prickles.

The genus name, *Hackelia*, honours 19th-century Czech botanist Josef Hackel. The species name, *floribunda*, means "producing many flowers." Indeed, a locally common name for the plant is Many-Flowered Stickseed. While the flowers on this plant are lovely to look at, the prickles on the nutlets cling easily to fur, feathers, and clothing, thus lending the plant its common name. The nutlets adhere to clothing like Velcro, and can be a huge nuisance in the late summer and autumn to anybody who walks close to the plant. The nutlets are tenacious and must be laboriously picked from socks, sweaters, and trousers. Long-haired hunting dogs can become covered in the nutlets, even to the extent that scissors are required to free the animal of the things. The nutlets are an extraordinarily effective mechanism for seed dispersal.

Tall Bluebells (Tall Lungwort)
Mertensia paniculata

BORAGE FAMILY

This perennial grows from a woody rootstock, is usually hairy, may have multiple branches, and grows up to 80 cm tall. The plant prefers moist woods, stream banks, shaded poplar groves, and mixed forests. The basal leaves are large, prominently veined, heart-shaped, white-hairy on both sides, and long-stalked. The stem leaves are stalkless or short-stalked, rounded at the base, and tapering to the pointed tip. The blue flowers occur in drooping clusters, hanging like small blue bells. The corolla is tubular, five-lobed, and abruptly enlarged in the middle. The flower buds often have a pinkish tinge, turning blue as they open.

The genus name, *Mertensia*, honours F.C. Mertens, an 18th-century German botanist. The common name, Lungwort, is derived from Europe, this plant's flowers being similar to the European Lungwort, a plant thought to be good in the treatment of lung diseases. Several related species occur in the region, but are uncommon. All are considerably smaller than this species, but all have the same flower conformation. Montana Bluebells is another common name that seems to be shared by all of the Mertensias.

One-Flowered Cancer Root (Naked Broomrape)
Orobanche uniflora

BROOMRAPE FAMILY

This plant is a saprophyte that gets its nourishment from decaying organic matter in the soil. It has no leaves, only scaly, whitish-tan bracts on the stem. The flower is solitary at the top of an unbranched 10 cm tall stem, tube-shaped, and violet to pale purple. The flower head is 2.5 cm long, and has five lobes of relatively equal size, each with three thin, dark stripes. Bright yellow-orange anthers are seen inside the throat of the flower. The plant grows at low to middle elevations, often in clumps.

The origin of the genus name, *Orobanche*, is discussed in the note on Clustered Broomrape (*O. fasciculata*), shown on page 110. The species name, *uniflora*, indicates only one flower per stem. The common name, Cancer Root, most probably is a reference to the parasitic nature of the plant. The plant is also known by the locally common names of Naked Broomrape and One-Flowered Broomrape. These common names arise because Scotch Broom (*Cytisus scoparius*) is often the host plant in Europe. In this region, the host plants are more usually those in the Stonecrop, Saxifrage, and Composite Families.

Blue Clematis
Clematis occidentalis

BUTTERCUP FAMILY

A plant of shaded riverine woods and thickets, the Clematis is a climbing, slightly hairy, reddish-stemmed vine that attaches itself to other plants by slender tendrils. The flowers have four to five sepals and are purplish to blue, with dark veins. The flowers resemble crepe paper. The fruits are mop-like clusters of seeds, each of which has a long feathery style.

The genus and common name is derived from the Greek word *klêma*, meaning "vine branch" or "tendril." The Blackfoot called the plant "ghost's lariat," a reference to the fact that the vine would entangle their feet when they walked through it. Many Native peoples used the plant to weave mats and bags. The whole plant is toxic if ingested. Clematis also occurs in yellow (*C. tangutica*), a naturalized variety. Western Clematis (*C. ligusticifolia*), shown on page 121, also occurs in the region. It has white flowers. Clematis often goes by the locally common name of Virgin's Bower.

Larkspur
Delphinium bicolor

BUTTERCUP FAMILY

This is a plant of open woods, grasslands, and slopes that grows up to 40 cm tall from fleshy rootstock. It usually has a single flowering stem. Larkspurs are easily recognized for their showy, highly modified flowers. The irregular petals are whitish to bluish, with sepals that are blue to violet. The upper sepal forms a large, hollow, nectar-producing spur. The flowers bloom up the stem in a loose, elongated cluster.

The genus name, *Delphinium*, is derived from the Greek word *delphini*, which means "dolphin," a reference to the plant's nectaries, which are said to resemble old pictures of dolphins. The common name is said to have originated because the spur on the flower resembles the spur on the foot of a lark. The plant is also known by the locally common names Little Larkspur and Montana Larkspur. The flowers are favoured by bumblebees and butterflies. The plant contains delphinine, a toxic alkaloid, and is poisonous to cattle and humans. Upland Larkspur (*D. nuttallianum*) is a similar species in the region. It is distinguished from this plant by having deep notches in the lowest two petals. Tall Larkspur (*D. glaucum*) also occurs in the region, but it is a large plant, growing up to 2 m tall. The flowers are similar in appearance to this species, and they are numerous and scattered up the plant in an elongated cluster.

Monkshood
Aconitum columbianum

BUTTERCUP FAMILY

A plant of moist mixed coniferous forests and meadows, Monkshood has a distinctive flower construction that is unmistakable. The dark blue to purple flowers appear in terminal, open clusters, and the sepals form a hood, like those worn by monks. The leaves are large, long-stalked, alternate and shaped like large maple leaves.

The genus name, *Aconitum*, is derived from the Greek *acon*, meaning "dart," a reference to the fact that arrows were often tipped with poison from this plant, the entire plant being poisonous. The plant contains alkaloids that can cause paralysis, decreased blood pressure and temperature, and can cause death within a few hours. The plant is also known by the locally common name Columbian Monkshood.

Prairie Crocus
Anemone patens (also *Pulsatilla patens*)

BUTTERCUP FAMILY

This plant is widespread and common in grasslands, dry meadows, and mountain slopes. It is usually one of the first wildflowers to bloom in the spring, and can occur in huge numbers. The flowers are usually solitary, various blues to purples in colour, and cup-shaped. White varieties are sometimes seen. It is interesting to note that the flower blooms before the basal leaves appear. The plant has many basal leaves, palmately divided into three main leaflets, and again divided into narrow linear segments. The leaves on the flower stem appear in a whorl of three. The fruits are large, spherical clusters of silky-haired, long-plumed seeds that are distributed by the wind.

The plant is also known as a Pasque Flower, *pasque* being an old French word for Easter, and referencing the blooming of this flower around the time of Easter. The texture of the petals is as soft as down. Prairie Crocus is the floral emblem of the Province of Manitoba. The plant contains a substance called protoanemonin, an irritant that can produce rashes.

Blue Lettuce
Lactuca tatarica ssp. *pulchella*

COMPOSITE FAMILY

This plant grows up to 1 m tall in fields, roadsides, meadows, shores, and stream banks, often found on moist, heavy soil. The leaves are hairless, lobed below, and simple above. The flowers are composite heads and have pale to dark blue ray florets, toothed at the tip. There are no disk florets.

The genus name, *Lactuca*, is derived from the Latin *lac*, meaning "milk," and refers to the milky sap the plant exudes when its stem is broken. The specific name, *tatarica*, apparently refers to the Tatars, a Turkic people of Russia, where a similar plant is known to exist. The subspecies name, *pulchella*, is derived from the Latin word for "beautiful." A similar introduced species, Prickly Lettuce (*L. serriola*) also exists in the region. It has yellow flowers. Plants of this genus are particularly enjoyed by horses, apparently, and they are sometimes referred to as Horseweeds.

Blue Sailors (Chicory)
Cichorium intybus

COMPOSITE FAMILY

This native of Eurasia grows up to 1.75 m tall at low elevations on dry plateaus, fields, grasslands and waste areas. The basal leaves are lance-shaped and strongly toothed to lobed. The flowers have sky blue ray flowers and no disk flowers, and they occur singly or in small groups widely spaced along the long branches, arising from the bases of the stem leaves. The flowers open only in the daylight. The stems exude a bitter-tasting, milky juice when broken.

The common name, Chicory, and the genus name are derived from the original Arabic name for wild chicory. The plant has long been used as food, and is known as Belgium Endive in the commercial vegetable trade. The leaves of this plant are eaten as a salad green, a practice dating back to the ancient Egyptians, and the roots are roasted and ground as a coffee substitute. The species name, *intybus*, is Latin, meaning "endive." The common name, Blue Sailors, is said to originate in a legend about a young woman who fell madly in love with a sailor. The sailor left her for his real love – the sea – and the woman was heart-broken and pitifully lonely. The gods took pity on her and changed her into a beautiful blue flower, thus Blue Sailors.

Showy Aster
Aster conspicuus

COMPOSITE FAMILY

This plant is widespread and common in low to middle elevations in moist to dry open forests, openings, clearings, and meadows. The flowers are few to many composite heads on glandular stalks, with 15 to 35 violet ray flowers and yellow disk flowers. The stem leaves are egg-shaped to elliptical, with sharp-toothed edges and clasping bases.

Aster is from the Latin word for "star," referring to the flower's shape. *Conspicuus* means "conspicuous," a reference to the showy flowers. Some Native peoples soaked the roots of the plant in water and used the decoction to treat boils. The leaves were also used as a poultice for that purpose.

Tall Purple Fleabane
Erigeron peregrinus

COMPOSITE FAMILY

This plant grows up to 70 cm tall from a thick rootstock, in the subalpine and alpine zones. The basal leaves are narrow and stemmed, while the stem leaves are smaller and stalkless. The flowers resemble daisies, with 30 to 80 rose- to purple-coloured ray florets, surrounding a yellow centre of disk florets. The large flowers are usually solitary, but there may be smaller flowers that appear from the axils of the upper leaves.

The origins of the common name, Fleabane, and the genus name, *Erigeron*, are discussed in the narrative on Daisy Fleabane (*E. compositus*), shown on page 130. This flower is sometimes referred to as Wandering Daisy.

Alpine Speedwell (Alpine Veronica)
Veronica wormskjoldii (also *V. alpina*)

FIGWORT FAMILY

This erect perennial stands up to 30 cm tall, and occurs in moist meadows and along streams in the subalpine and alpine zones. The leaves are elliptic to egg-shaped, and occur in opposite pairs, spaced along the stem. The stems, leaves, and stalks of the flowers are covered with fine, sticky hairs. The flowers are numerous and occur at the top of the stem. The corolla has four united blue petals, which exhibit dark veins.

The genus name, *Veronica*, honours Saint Veronica. According to the canonization, Veronica took pity on Jesus when he was carrying his cross to Golgotha (Calvary), and she used her kerchief to wipe sweat from his face. When the kerchief came back to her, it was impressed with an image of his face – the *vera iconica* or "true likeness." The sacred relic was kept in St. Peter's in the Vatican, but the name was applied to the genus to link Saint Veronica to a common flower often seen by the pious public. The species name, *wormskjoldii*, honours Morton Wormskjold, an 18th-century Danish naturalist. The common name, Speedwell, is said to come from the old English blessing or benediction "god speed," though why the name is applied to flowers of this genus is unknown.

Fuzzy-Tongued Penstemon
Penstemon eriantherus

FIGWORT FAMILY

This perennial grows up to 40 cm tall from a taproot on dry, open slopes from valleys to the montane zone, and is generally restricted to the southeastern part of the region. The plant is grey-hairy overall. The basal and lower stem leaves are opposite, usually entire, lance- to egg-shaped, and stalked. The upper leaves are lance-shaped to oblong and more or less unstalked. The inflorescence is a terminal cluster of several whorls of stalked, tubular flowers that flare at the mouth. The flowers are pale lavender to blue-purple, with lines of a darker colour inside. They are strongly two-lipped, with the upper lip being two-lobed and the lower lip being three-lobed and longer than the upper lip. The flower is strongly bearded inside the throat, thus the common name.

The origin of the genus name, *Penstemon*, is discussed in the note on Small-Flowered Penstemon (*P. procerus*), shown on page 84. The species name, *eriantherus*, means "woolly flowered," a reference to the overall hairy appearance of the plant. The long, tubular flowers are often pollinated by bees and hummingbirds. Indeed, I have seen bees absolutely disappear briefly as they enter the flower, then back out covered in pollen.

Shrubby Penstemon (Shrubby Beardtongue)
Penstemon fruticosus

FIGWORT FAMILY

V. Skilton

Virginia Skilton image

This plant grows in dry areas from the montane to the subalpine zones. It has woody stems and almost appears to be a shrub growing to 40 cm tall, hence the common name. The leaves are opposite, lance-shaped, shiny, and evergreen, with the largest leaves appearing at the base of the stem. The flowers are large and lavender to purplish-blue. The flowers appear in a raceme in pairs on one side of the stem.

The origin of the common name, Beardtongue, and the genus name, *Penstemon,* are discussed in the note on Small-Flowered Penstemon (*P. procerus*), shown on page 84. Native peoples often added the leaves and flowers of this plant to cooking pits to flavour wild onions and Balsamroot. The long, tubular flowers are often pollinated by bees and hummingbirds. Meriwether Lewis collected a specimen of this plant in 1806 along the Lolo Trail in present-day Idaho on the return of the party from wintering on the Columbia River. The plant is also known by the locally common name Bush Penstemon.

Small-Flowered Penstemon (Slender Beardtongue)
Penstemon procerus

FIGWORT FAMILY

This plant grows to 40 cm tall at low to alpine elevations, usually in dry to moist open forests, grassy clearings, meadows, and disturbed areas. Most of the blunt to lance-shaped leaves appear in opposite pairs up the stem. The flowers are small, funnel-shaped, blue to purple, and appear in one to several tight clusters arranged in whorls around the stem and at its tip.

The common name, Beardtongue, describes the hairy, tongue-like staminode (sterile stamen) in the throat of the flower. The genus name, *Penstemon*, originates from the Greek *pente*, meaning "five," and *stemon*, meaning "stamen," five being the total number of stamens in the flower. The genus is a large and complex group of plants. There are many different Penstemons in the region, and often they will hybridize freely, adding even more confusion to the specific identification. This plant can usually be identified by its small, tightly packed blue flowers that appear in whorls around the stem, often in interrupted clusters. The species name, *procerus*, is derived from Latin and means "very tall," which is somewhat peculiar because this plant is not usually very tall. Other common names applied to the plant are Slender Beardtongue, Slender Blue Beardtongue, and Small-Flowered Beardtongue.

Blue Flax
Linum lewisii

FLAX FAMILY

This perennial grows from a woody base and taproot up to 60 cm tall on dry, exposed hillsides, grasslands, roadsides, and gravelly river flats. The leaves are alternate, simple, and stalkless. The flowers have five petals, five sepals, five styles, and five stamens. The flowers are pale purplish-blue, with darkish guidelines, yellowish at the base, and appear on very slender stems that are constantly moving, even with the smallest of breezes.

The genus name, *Linum*, is derived from the Greek *linon*, meaning "thread." The plant has been cultivated for various uses, notably oil and linen, since ancient times. This species was first described for science by Frederick Pursh in his book *Flora Americae Septentrionalis* from a specimen collected by Meriwether Lewis in 1806 at the Sun River in present-day Montana, and it bears his name. Some Native peoples used the seeds from the plant as food. They also used the plant medicinally as a poultice to reduce swelling. The stem fibres were used in the manufacture of cordage. The common name, Flax, is derived from the Latin *filum*, which means "thread."

Northern Gentian
Gentianella amarella (also *Gentiana amarella*)

GENTIAN FAMILY

This is a plant of moist places in meadows, woods, ditches, and stream banks, up to the subalpine zone. These lovely flowers are first sighted by their star-like formation winking at the top of the corolla tube, amidst adjacent grasses. The plant is most often small, standing only 15–20 cm, though taller specimens are sometimes seen. The flowers appear in clusters in the axils of the upper stem leaves, the leaves being opposite and appearing almost to be small hands holding up the flowers for inspection. There is a fringe inside the throat of the flower.

The genus name, *Gentianella*, comes from Gentius, a king of ancient Illyria, a coastal region on the Adriatic Sea. Gentius was said to have discovered medicinal properties in the plants of this genus. Gentians have been used as medicinal tonics for centuries. The species name, amarella, is derived from the Latin amarus, meaning "bitter," a reference to the bitter alkaloids contained in the plant's juices. The plant is also commonly referred to as Autumn Dwarf Gentian and Felwort. The latter name is derived from Old English *feld*, which means "field," and *wort*, which means "herb" or "a plant." Flowers in the genus *Gentianella* do not have pleats between the petal lobes. Flowers in the related genus *Gentiana* do have a pleat between the petal lobes and lack the fringe in the throat of the flower.

Sticky Purple Geranium
Geranium viscosissimum

GERANIUM FAMILY

This is a plant of moist grasslands, open woods, and thickets that can grow up to 60 cm tall. The flowers have large, showy, rose-purple to bluish petals that are strongly veined with purple. The long-stalked leaves are deeply lobed, and split into five to seven sharply toothed divisions appearing in opposite pairs along the stem. There are sticky, glandular hairs covering the stems, leaves, and some flower parts. The fruit is an elongated, glandular-hairy capsule, with a long beak, shaped like a stork's or crane's bill.

The genus name, *Geranium*, is derived from the Greek *geranos*, meaning "crane," a reference to the fruit being shaped like a crane's bill. Indeed, Crane's Bill is an oft-used common name for the Geraniums and some people call this plant Sticky Purple Crane's Bill. The species name, *viscosissimum*, is the Latin superlative for viscid, which means "thick and gluey." The sticky, glandular hairs appearing on the stems and leaves effectively protect the plant from pollen theft by ants and other crawling insects. The Sticky Purple Geranium is very similar to a European import that has naturalized in dry grasslands in western North America — the Stork's Bill (*Erodium cicutarium*). Interestingly enough, *Erodium* is Greek for "heron," another bird with a long, pointed bill. The ornithological references to storks, herons, and cranes can certainly lead to some confusion when common names are applied to wildflowers of the Geranium Family.

Harebell
Campanula rotundifolia

HAREBELL FAMILY

This plant is widespread in a variety of habitats, including grasslands, gullies, moist forests, openings, clearings and rocky open ground. The flowers are purplish-blue, rarely white, bell-shaped, with hairless sepals, nodding on a thin stem in loose clusters. The leaves are thin on the stem and lance-shaped. The basal leaves are heart-shaped and coarsely toothed, but they usually wither before the flowers appear.

The genus name, *Campanula*, is derived from the Latin *campana*, meaning "bell." *Campanula* is the diminutive of *campana*, thus "little bell." The species name, *rotundifolia*, refers to the round basal leaves. This is the Bluebell of Scotland, and one school of thought holds that Harebell comes from a contraction of "heatherbell." Another school of thought holds that Harebell is a misspelling of "hairbell," the reference being to the hair-thin stems on which the flowers appear. Where Harebells occur, they can be in profusion and can cast a purple hue to the area when they are in bloom. The Cree were said to have chopped and dried the roots to make into compresses for stopping bleeding and to reduce swelling. The foliage contains alkaloids and is avoided by browsing animals. Mountain Harebell (C. *lasiocarpa*), also known as Alpine Harebell, is an allied species found in the region. It occurs at high subalpine to alpine elevations, and has a large, solitary, bell-shaped flower that blooms low to the ground.

Blue-Eyed Grass
Sisyrinchium montanum

IRIS FAMILY

These beautiful flowers can be found scattered among the grasses of moist meadows from the prairies to the subalpine zones. The distinctively flattened stems grow to 30 cm tall, and are twice as tall as the grass-like basal leaves. The blue flower is star-shaped, with three virtually identical petals and sepals, each tipped with a minute point. There is a bright yellow eye in the centre of the flower. The blossoms are very short-lived, wilting usually within one day, to be replaced by fresh ones the next day.

The genus name, *Sisyrinchium*, was a name applied by Theophrastus, a disciple of Aristotle who refined the philosopher's work in botany and natural sciences in ancient Greece. It is a reference to a plant allied to the Iris. The species name, *montanum*, is Latin meaning "of the mountains," though indeed the plant is also found in other environments. The flower has a number of locally common names, including Montana Blue-Eyed Grass, Idaho Blue-Eyed Grass, Eyebright, Grass Widow, and Blue Star.

Chocolate Lily (Checker Lily)
Fritillaria affinis (formerly *F. lanceolata*)

LILY FAMILY

This early-blooming upright perennial grows up to 80 cm tall in variable habitat that includes prairies, grassy bluffs, woodlands, and conifer forests from low elevations to the montane zone. The plant grows from a cluster of bulbs and small offsets that resemble grains of rice. Indeed, a locally common name for the plant is Rice Root. The narrow, lance-shaped leaves are up to 15 cm long, and all are borne on the stem, mostly arranged in one or two imperfect whorls of three to five leaves. Several nodding flowers occur in a loose raceme up the stem. Each individual flower has six purple tepals, checked with yellow, giving the flower a dark brown appearance, and giving rise to another common name, Chocolate Lily. The flowers are ill-scented, described variously as smelling of rotten meat or dirty socks. This foul odour is probably an allure to flies as pollinators.

The genus name, *Fritillaria*, is derived from the Latin *fritillus*, which means "dice box," most probably a reference to the fruit, which appears as an erect, cylindrical capsule. The first specimen collected for science was gathered by Meriwether Lewis in April 1806 on the Columbia River in what is now the State of Oregon. Mission Bells is another locally common name applied to the plant. Yellowbell (*F. pudica*), shown on page 41, is a closely related species that occurs in the region. It has yellow bell-shaped flowers.

Early Camas
Camassia quamash

LILY FAMILY

This plant of wet meadows and stream banks has long, narrow grass-like leaves, and a tall, naked stem. The startling blue to purplish flowers are numerous, and appear in a loose cluster at the top of the stem. The flowers have six tepals that are spreading and somewhat unevenly spaced. The stamens are golden, and contrast vividly with the blue inflorescence of the plant.

The genus and species names for this plant are derived from the names given to the plant by the Nimi'-pu, or Nez Perce people. In September 1805, Captain William Clark of the Lewis and Clark expedition, came upon some Nez Perce digging the bulbs of the plant for food. The Nez Perce shared the bulbs with the members of the expedition, at a time when food had grown scarce for the expedition. The onion-like bulbs were a very important food for Native peoples, trappers, and settlers in western North America. The bulbs were baked, boiled, roasted, eaten raw, and ground into flour for baking bread. So important were the bulbs, that local wars were fought over the rights to certain large meadows where the plants grew in profusion. Victoria, British Columbia, was once called Camosun, meaning "a place for gathering camas."

Heal-All (Self-Heal)
Prunella vulgaris

MINT FAMILY

This is a plant found in moist woods, along stream banks and lakeshores and in fields from the prairie to the montane zone. The flowers occur in terminal clusters, usually surrounded by the upper leaves. The bracts are kidney-shaped to oval, with spines at the tips and hairs along the margins. The few leaves are opposite, smooth and sparsely hairy. The plant is small and sprawling, and square-stemmed.

The genus name, *Prunella*, is most likely derived from the German *bräune*, meaning "quinsy," or angina tonsillaris, a condition this plant was used to cure. The traditional use of the plant for healing internal and external bleeding gives rise to the common names, but tests on the plant's extracts have not revealed any biochemical basis for the claims of healing. Parts of this small flower have been used by Native peoples to relieve boils, cuts, bruises, swellings and internal bleeding. The Cree treated sore throats with an extract from the plant. The Blackfoot used it as an eyewash and treated horses' saddle sores with it. The leaves can be brewed into a tea.

Marsh Skullcap
Scutellaria galericulata

MINT FAMILY

This member of the mint family grows up to 80 cm tall at low to middle elevations in wetlands, along lakeshores, on stream banks, and in ditches. The leaves are opposite, oval to lance-shaped, and are irregularly scalloped along the blades. The stem is square, typical of the mint family. The trumpet-shaped flowers have a hooded upper lip and a broad, hairless lower lip, and are blue to purplish-pink marked with white. The flowers occur as solitary on slender stalks or as pairs in the leaf axils.

The genus name, *Scutellaria*, is derived from the Latin *scutella*, which means "a small dish, tray, saucer or platter," a reference to the appearance of the sepals during fruiting. The species name, *galericulata,* means "helmet shaped." The common name for the plant comes from the hood-like appearance of the upper lip of the flower. The plant contains a flavonoid called scutellaria that has sedative and anti-spasmodic properties. A tea made from the plant has long been used by herbalists to treat nervous disorders.

Wild Mint (Canada Mint)
Mentha arvensis (also *M. canadensis*)

MINT FAMILY

This plant inhabits wetland marshes, moist woods, banks and shores of streams and lakes, and sometimes lives in shallow water. The purplish, to pinkish, to bluish flowers are crowded in dense clusters in the upper leaf axils. The leaves are opposite, prominently veined, and highly scented of mint if crushed. The stems are square in cross-section and hairy.

The genus name, *Mentha*, is from the Greek *Minthe*, a mythological nymph loved by Pluto. A jealous Proserpine changed the nymph into a mint plant. The species name, *arvensis*, means "of cultivated fields." The strong, distinctive taste of mint plants is from their volatile oils. The leaves have long been used fresh, dried, and frozen as a flavouring and for teas. Some Native peoples used the leaves to flavour meat and pemmican, and lined dried-meat containers with mint leaves prior to winter storage. Strong mint teas were used by Native peoples and European settlers as a treatment for coughs, colds, and fevers. Wild Mint often occurs in extensive patches.

Dame's Rocket (Dame's Violet)
Hesperis matronalis

MUSTARD FAMILY

This member of the mustard family was introduced from Eurasia into North America during colonial days as an ornamental plant, and it has spread extensively, now being found throughout Canada and much of the United States. In many areas it is looked upon as an invasive, noxious weed, though it is still available and sold as an ornamental by some nurseries. Typically it inhabits disturbed sites, waste ground, thickets, woods, and road and railsides. The plant is erect and grows to over 1 m tall. The leaves are alternate, lance-shaped, predominantly clasping on the stem, hairy on both sides, and become progressively smaller up the stem. The flowers occur in showy clusters at the top of the stem. Each flower is four-petalled, purple to blue to white, and fragrant.

The genus name, *Hesperis*, is derived from the Greek *hesperos*, which means "evening," the reference being that the flowers are said to have an enhanced aroma near evening. The species name, *matronalis*, is said to derive from the flower being a favourite of Roman matrons, ergo the reference to Dame in the common name. Dame's Rocket goes by a number of other common names, including Dame's Violet, Dames Wort, Sweet Rocket, and Mother of the Evening.

Alfalfa
Medicago sativa

PEA FAMILY

Alfalfa is an introduced species that was brought to North America as a forage crop for livestock. It has escaped from cultivated fields and is now locally common in roadside ditches and rights-of-way. The leaves are elliptic to oblong, and occur in threes. They are slightly hairy, and sharply toothed at the tips. The flowers are pea-like, purple to blue, and occur in oblong-shaped clusters. The fruits are spirally coiled pods.

Alfalfa is said to have been cultivated as far back in history as the Medes in ancient Persia. The Greeks introduced the plant to Europe at the time of the Persian wars. Black Medick (*M. lupulina*) is a close relative of Alfalfa found in the same habitat. Black Medick has yellow flowers, and its fruit is less tightly coiled than Alfalfa's and turns black at maturity. Alfalfa is similar to another common introduced species, Sweet-Clover (*Melilotus* spp.), but Alfalfa generally has narrower and more wedge-shaped leaves that are toothed only near the tip.

Bladder Locoweed (Stalked-Pod Crazyweed)
Oxytropis podocarpa

PEA FAMILY

This alpine plant grows high above timberline on gravelly slopes, from a stout taproot that produces a rosette of leaves that lie flat on the ground. The leaves are covered with silvery hairs, and consist of 11 to 23 short, linear leaflets. The flower stalks are leafless, and rise just above the leaves, terminating with two or three pale purple, pea-like flowers about 2 cm long. Each flower has a dark purple, hairy calyx, with a characteristic beaked keel formed from the two lower fused petals. This beaked keel distinguishes members of this genus from those of the Milk-Vetches (*Astragalus*). The fruits are inflated, egg-shaped pods, up to 3 cm long, that turn bright red to purple in the fall. A style remains attached to the pointed end of the pod.

The genus name, *Oxytropis*, is derived from the Greek *oxys*, which means "sharp," and *tropis*, which means "keel," a reference to the beaked keel on the flowers in this genus. The species name, *podocarpa*, means "stalked fruits," a reference to the inflated pods of the plant. *Oxytropis* is the genus that contains Locoweeds, and indeed this plant is sometimes referred to as Stalked-Pod Crazyweed or Inflated Oxytropis. Plants of this genus contain poisonous alkaloids that can cause the blind staggers in animals that consume them, hence the reference to loco or crazy.

Silky Lupine
Lupinus sericeus

PEA FAMILY

A leafy, erect, tufted perennial with stout stems that appears in sandy to gravelly grasslands, open woods, and roadsides, often growing in dense clumps or bunches. The plant grows up to 80 cm tall. The flowers are showy in dense, long, terminal clusters, and display a variety of colours in blues and purples, occasionally white and yellow. Tremendous colour variation can occur, even in plants that are very close to one another. Flowers have a typical pea shape, with a strongly truncated keel and a pointed tip. The leaves of Lupines are very distinctive. They are palmately compound and alternate on the stem, with five to nine very narrow leaflets that have silky hairs on both sides.

The genus name, *Lupinus*, is Latin meaning "of or belonging to a wolf." That much appears to be accepted, but how this name came to be applied to this plant is open to contention. Perhaps the best explanation is that the plants were once thought (inaccurately) to be a devourer or robber of soil nutrients, hence a wolf. In fact, the root nodules of Lupines produce a nitrogen-fixing bacteria that actually tends to enrich poor soil. The species name, *sericeus*, is from the Latin *sericus*, meaning "silken," a reference to the soft, silky hairs that cover the plant. The fruits of Lupine contain an alkaloid, and may be poisonous to some livestock, particularly sheep. Dwarf Mountain Lupine (L. *lyallii*) is a related subalpine and alpine species. It only grows to 10 cm tall, and has purple flowers with a white stripe on the central part of the banner.

Tufted Vetch (Bird Vetch)
Vicia cracca

PEA FAMILY

This plant thrives in shady riverine habitats, open woods, thickets, and meadows. The purple flowers are typical of the pea family. The leaves are alternate, pinnately divided, and have forked tendrils at the ends of the leaves. The plant creeps and climbs over adjacent plants.

The genus name, *Vicia*, is derived from the Latin *vincire*, which means "to bind together," referring to the binding tendrils on the leaves. *Vicia* was apparently translated to Old North French as *veche*, and later became the English word *vetch*. The species name, *cracca*, is the Latin name for Vetch. Vetches can build nitrates in soil and are looked upon as good forage for livestock. Vetches are sometimes difficult to differentiate from peas (genus *Lathyrus*). The flower in question must be examined closely, perhaps even under low magnification. Pinch the keel to expose the pistil. In Vetches the style has hairs arranged all around, like a bottle brush; in peas the style has hairs only on one side, like a toothbrush.

Jacob's Ladder (Showy Jacob's Ladder)
Polemonium pulcherrimum

PHLOX FAMILY

This beautiful plant grows in dry, open, rocky environments in the montane to alpine zones. The leaves are distinctive. They are pinnately compound, with 11 to 25 round to elliptic leaflets that are evenly spaced to resemble a tiny ladder. The leaf arrangement gives the plant its common name – a reference to the story in the Bible book of Genesis wherein Jacob found a ladder to heaven. The pale to dark blue, cup-shaped flowers appear in an open cluster at the top of the stem. The flowers have a vivid orange ring at the base of the cup. The plant is covered with glandular hairs, which are said to impart the foul odour of the plant.

There are two schools of thought as to the origin of the genus name, *Polemonium*. One school holds that the name comes from the Greek philosopher Polemon. The other holds that the name is derived from the Greek word *polemos*, which means "strife." According to this school of thought, a dispute as to who discovered the plant, and its supposed medicinal properties, sparked a war between two kings! The species name is the superlative of the Latin adjective *pulcher*, which means "beautiful" or "handsome." The plant is apparently a favourite of bees.

Shooting Star
Dodecatheon pulchellum

PRIMROSE FAMILY

This beautiful plant is scattered and locally common at low to alpine elevations in warm, dry climates, grasslands, mountain meadows, and stream banks. The leaves are lance- to spatula-shaped, and appear in a basal rosette. The flowers appear, one to several, nodding atop a leafless stalk. The flowers are purple to lavender, occasionally white, with corolla lobes turned backward. The stamens are united into a yellow to orange tube, from which the style and anthers protrude.

A harbinger of spring, these lovely flowers bloom in huge numbers, and the grasslands take on a purple hue when the Shooting Stars are in bloom. The genus name, *Dodecatheon*, is derived from the Greek *dodeka*, meaning "twelve," and *theos*, meaning "gods," thus a plant that is protected by twelve gods. The species name, *pulchellum*, is Latin for "beautiful." Native peoples used an infusion from this plant as an eyewash, and some looked upon the plant as a charm to obtain wealth. Some tribes mashed the flowers to make a pink dye for their arrows. The common name is an apt description of the flower, with the turned-back petals streaming behind the stamens.

Marsh Cinquefoil
Potentilla palustris

ROSE FAMILY

This plant inhabits bogs, marshes, streams, and ponds from the valleys to the subalpine zone. It grows from long, smooth rhizomes, creeping along the ground and rooting at the nodes. The leaves are usually smooth and pinnately compound, with five to seven obovate (teardrop shaped) leaflets that are deeply toothed. While other members of the *Potentilla* family have yellow or white/cream coloured flowers, Marsh Cinquefoil has purple to deep red flowers.

The origin of the genus name, *Potentilla*, is explained in the note on Silverweed (*P. anserina*), shown on page 58. The species name, *palustris,* is derived from the Latin *palus*, which means "marsh" or "swamp," a reference to the favoured habitat of the plant. The flowers have an offensive, rotten odour that attracts insects as pollinators. The plant is also known by the locally common name Purple Marshlocks.

Purple Saxifrage (Purple Mountain Saxifrage)
Saxifraga oppositifolia

SAXIFRAGE FAMILY

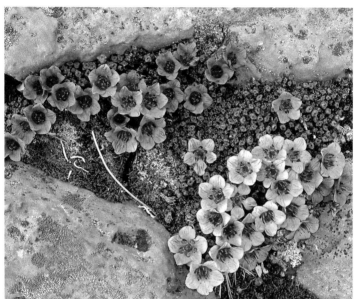

Tracy Utting image

This plant is a very low, matted, cushion-forming plant, with tightly packed stems, common to the rocky talus slopes, ledges, and boulder fields in the alpine zone, particularly on calcium-rich substrates. The five-petalled purple to pink flowers appear singly on short stems. The leaves are opposite, stalkless, and appear whorled. Each leaf is broadly wedge-shaped, and bluish-green.

The origin of the genus name, *Saxifraga*, is discussed in the note on Alaska Saxifrage (*S. ferruginea*), shown on page 210. The species name, *oppositifolia*, refers to the opposite arrangement of the leaves. The plant blooms early in the year, and given its blooming time and its somewhat inaccessible habitat, it is often gone before it is seen by many people. Purple Saxifrage is the official flower of the Territory of Nunavut.

Early Blue Violet (Western Long-Spurred Violet)
Viola adunca

VIOLET FAMILY

A plant of the grasslands, open woods, and slopes, this violet is widespread in North America and is highly variable. The flower colour ranges from blue to purple, and the three lower petals are often whitish at the base, pencilled with darker purple guidelines. The largest petal has a hooked spur half as long as the lower petal. The leaves are mostly basal, oval with a heart-shaped base, and have round teeth on the margins. The plant grows low to the ground.

The genus name, *Viola,* is derived from the Latin *violaceous,* for the purple colour of many members of the genus. The species name, *adunca,* means "hooked," a reference to the hook on the spur of the flower. An *uncus* was a hook used by the Romans to drag executed bodies away from the place of execution. Violets have been used for food for centuries. The leaves are high in vitamins A and C, and can be used to make a bland tea. Violet seeds have special oily bodies called elaiosomes, which attract ants. The ants carry the seeds away to their nests, thus dispersing the seeds. Common garden Pansies are also a member of the *Viola* genus.

Ballhead Waterleaf
Hydrophyllum capitatum

WATERLEAF FAMILY

This perennial grows from a deep rhizome that puts up one or more hairy, spreading to ascending stems up to 40 cm tall in woodlands and on open slopes from valleys to subalpine elevations. The leaves are mostly basal, long-stalked, 15 cm long and half as wide, and pinnately divided into 7 to 11 leaflets with round margins. The inflorescence occurs in compact, short-stalked, rounded clusters of funnel-shaped lavender to bluish-purple flowers. The individual flowers are five-lobed, and the styles and stamens protrude from the flowers, giving the inflorescence a fuzzy appearance. The clusters of flowers are usually shorter than the leaves, appearing to hide under the leaves.

The genus name, *Hydrophyllum*, is derived from the Greek *hydro*, which means "water," and *phyllon*, which means "leaf," a literal translation of the genus name which is most probably a reference to the succulent leaves of members of the genus. The specific name, *capitatum*, is Latin and refers to the way the flowers form a head-like cluster. Some Native peoples used the roots of the plant as food, while others used it medicinally as a cure for diarrhea. The plant also goes by the locally common name of Woolen Britches. Fendler's Waterleaf (*H. fendleri*), is a related species that occurs in the region. It usually has white flowers. Pacific Waterleaf (*H. tenuipes*), also has white flowers, but it appears west of the coastal ranges.

Silky Phacelia (Silky Scorpionweed)
Phacelia sericea

WATERLEAF FAMILY

This plant grows on dry, rocky, open slopes at moderate to high elevations. The leaves are deeply divided into many segments and covered with silky hairs. The purple to blue flowers occur in clusters up a spike, resembling a bottle brush. The individual flowers are funnel-shaped, with long, purple, yellow-tipped stamens sticking out. The clusters of coiled branches resemble scorpion tails, thus the common name.

The genus name, *Phacelia*, is derived from the Greek *phakelos*, meaning "bundle," a reference to the dense flower clusters. The species name, *sericea*, means "silky," a reference to the fine hairs on the plant. Some people experience a dermatological reaction if they handle the plant. This plant is a spectacular find while hiking. Once seen it will not be forgotten.

Thread-Leaved Phacelia (Thread-Leaved Scorpionweed)
Phacelia linearis

WATERLEAF FAMILY

This annual species of *Phacelia* grows to 50 cm tall, and appears on dry plateaus and foothills in the region. The leaves are hairy, alternate, thin and linear below, developing side lobes higher on the stem. The flowers are reasonably large, lavender to blue and appearing in open clusters from the leaf axils.

The origin of the genus name, *Phacelia*, is discussed in the note on Silky Phacelia (*P. sericea*), shown on page 106. The common name, Scorpionweed, arises because some people say the coiled branches of the flower clusters resemble the tail of a scorpion. The first specimen of the species was collected by Meriwether Lewis in the spring of 1806 near present-day The Dalles, Oregon.

White, Green, and Brown Flowers

This section includes flowers that are predominantly white or cream coloured, green, or brown when encountered in the field. Given that some flowers fade to other colours as they age, if you do not find the flower you are looking for in this section, check the other sections in the book.

Sitka Alder

Alnus crispa ssp. *sinuata* (also *A. viridis* ssp. *sinuata*)

BIRCH FAMILY

This deciduous shrub grows up to 5 m tall, and is commonly found from low elevations to timberline in forests, clearings, and seepage areas. The leaves are broadly oval, with rounded bases, pointed tips, and double-toothed margins. The male and female flowers develop with the leaves. The male catkins are long and drooping; the female catkins are short and cone-like.

Alnus is the classical Latin name for the genus. The species name, *crispa*, is derived from Latin and means "curled" or "wavy," a reference to the leaf margins of the species. Somewhat redundantly, the subspecies name, *sinuata*, also means "bend, wind, curve, bow, swell out in curves." Native peoples made extensive use of the plant as fuel, as basket-making material, and for smoking fish and meat. They also extracted a reddish dye from the plant. Alders improve soil fertility by fixing nitrogen in nodules on their roots.

Clustered Broomrape

Orobanche fasciculata

BROOMRAPE FAMILY

Virginia Skilton image

This plant is a parasitic perennial that grows to 15 cm tall in grasslands and dry open forests, often using sagebrushes (*Artemisia* spp.) as host plants. The "leaves" on the plant are brownish scales. The flower stalks are fleshy, glandular-hairy, brown, and often yellowish or purple tinged. Three to ten flowers appear atop the stalks. The flowers have a purplish or yellowish tube-shaped corolla, with two lips, the upper being two-lobed, and the lower three-lobed.

The common name, Broomrape, comes from a related English species that is parasitic on Scotch Broom (*Cytisus scoparius*). The genus name, *Orobanche*, is derived from the Greek *orobos*, which means "clinging plant," and *ancho*, which means "to strangle," a reference to the plant's parasitic growth habit. The species name, *fasciculata*, is derived from the Latin *fascis*, which means "clustered" or "bundled," a reference to the bunched nature of the flowers. These plants get their nutrients from the host plant, and therefore have no need for photosynthesis. It is no doubt overstating the case to imply that these plants are strangling or doing other violence to their host plants.

Buck-Bean (Bog-Bean)
Menyanthes trifoliata

BUCK-BEAN FAMILY

Jim Riley image

This perennial is an aquatic to semi-aquatic plant that grows up to 30 cm tall from a thick, scaly, creeping rootstock. It appears in swampy land, bogs, ditches, and lake and pond margins. The leaves are basal, clasping, long-stemmed, and compound, with three smooth, elliptical, shiny, green leaflets. The leafless flowering stems arise from the leaves and hold crowded clusters of white flowers at their ends. The flowers are whitish inside, pink to purplish outside, and have a tube-shaped, five-part corolla, densely bearded inside.

The genus name, *Menyanthes*, is said to originate from the Greek *mene*, which means "month," and *anthos*, which means "flower," said to be a reference to the length of time of blooming of the plant. The species name, *trifoliata*, refers to the three-parted leaves. Some Native peoples used the rhizomes of the plant as famine food. They also brewed a tea made from the leaves and used it medicinally for a variety of aliments, including migraine headaches, fevers, and indigestion. The whole plant is also browsed by ungulates. The reference to Bean in the common name is a mystery, this plant bearing no relation whatsoever to beans by way of leaf, flower, or fruit.

Snow Brush (Sticky Laurel)
Ceanothus velutinus

BUCKTHORN FAMILY

This erect evergreen shrub grows to 2 m tall on well-drained slopes in the montane and subalpine forests, and is abundant after a forest fire. The aromatic leaves are alternate and oval, finely toothed, dark green on the top, greyish and smooth underneath. A varnish-like sticky substance covers the upper leaf surface, giving it a shiny appearance and a strong aroma. The leaves have three prominent veins that radiate from the leaf base. The flowers bloom in the early summer, and are tiny and white, heavily scented, and occur in dense clusters on stalks at the ends of the branches.

The genus name, Ceanothus, is derived from the Greek *keanothus*, a name given to an unrelated Old World spiny plant. Deer and elk often browse on this plant in the winter. The leaves and stems of the plant contain a toxic glucoside – saponin – but ungulates seem to suffer no ill effects from eating the plant. The seeds of the plant are impervious to moisture and can survive in the forest duff for up to three centuries. The seeds require either heat or scarification to germinate, so young shrubs grow rapidly after a fire, but are eventually shaded out by trees. The locally common name Sticky Laurel arises because of the sticky leaves resembling those of laurel (*Kalmia* spp.). The plant is also known as Hooker's Ceanothus. Buckbrush (*C. sanguineus*), also known as Redstem Ceanothus, is an allied plant that occurs in similar habitat. It is deciduous, and its leaves lack the sticky substance found on the leaves of Snow Brush.

Alpine Bistort (Viviparous Knotweed)
Polygonum viviparum

BUCKWHEAT FAMILY

This plant grows up to 30 cm tall, and is found in moist meadows and along stream banks in the subalpine and alpine zones. The leaves are basal, lance-shaped, dark green, and shiny. The flowers are small, white (sometimes pink), and occur in a cluster at the top of an upright spike. The lower flowers give way to small purplish bulblets, each of which is capable of producing a new plant – whether dislodged from the stem or indeed still attached to the parent plant. These bulblets actually germinate while still attached to the parent plant.

The origin of the common name, Knotweed, and the genus name, *Polygonum*, is discussed in the note on Water Smartweed (*P. amphibium*), shown on page 231. Some Native peoples viewed this root as snake-like in appearance, and that led some to believe that Bistort might be an anti-venom for snake bite. The species name, *viviparum*, is Latin meaning "producing or bringing forth live young," a reference to the bulblets of the plant. Some Native peoples used the roots and leaves as food.

Cushion Buckwheat (Silver-Plant)
Eriogonum ovalifolium

BUCKWHEAT FAMILY

This mat-forming species can be found from prairie elevations to the alpine ridges. The sometimes large mats of the plant are distinctive and appealing to the eye on high rocky ridges. The leaves are oval in shape and densely covered in silver woolly hairs, giving the plant an overall grey or silver appearance. The white to cream-coloured flowers occur in dense, rounded heads atop short, leafless stems that arise from the basal growth. A plant may have numerous such flowering stems. The flower umbels in this species are simple, not compound as in most members of the genus.

The genus name, *Eriogonum*, is derived from the Greek *erion*, which means "wool," and *gonu*, which means "knee" or "joint," a reference to the woolly, jointed stems of many members of the genus. The flowers of this genus usually have an unpleasant smell, but the nectar appears to be relished by bees, and produces a strongly flavoured, buckwheat-like honey.

Sulphur Buckwheat
Eriogonum umbellatum

BUCKWHEAT FAMILY

This perennial grows from a stout taproot and tends to be mat forming. The leaves are all basal. They are spoon- to egg-shaped, narrowing to a slender stalk, greenish above and often woolly white below. The leaves turn bright red in the fall. The flowering stem is usually leafless and up to 30 cm tall. The stem supports an inflorescence composed of small creamy white to pale yellow flowers that are held in compact spherical clusters (umbels). The flowers are sometimes tinged with pink on aging. The plant occurs from moderate to alpine elevations on grassy slopes, dry gravel ridges, alpine ridges, and talus slopes.

The origin of the genus name, *Eriogonum*, is explained in the note on Cushion Buckwheat (*E. ovalifolium*), shown on page 114. The specific name, *umbellatum*, is a reference to the shape of the inflorescence, and indeed this plant also goes by the locally common name Sub-Alpine Umbrellaplant. The flowers of this genus usually have an unpleasant smell, but the nectar appears to be relished by bees, and produces a strongly flavoured, buck-wheat-like honey.

Baneberry
Actaea rubra

BUTTERCUP FAMILY

This perennial grows up to 1 m tall in moist shady woods and thickets, along streams, and in clearings from low to subalpine elevations. The plant has one to several stout, upright, branching stems. The leaves are all on the stem. They are divided two or three times into threes, and are coarsely toothed. The inflorescence is a dense, white, cone-shaped cluster of flowers that appears on top of a spike. The fruit is a large cluster of either shiny red or white berries. At the time of flowering, there is no way to determine whether the berries of a particular plant will be red or white.

The common name of the plant is derived from the Anglo-Saxon word *bana*, meaning "murderer" or "destroyer" – undoubtedly a reference to the fact that the leaves, roots and berries of this plant are extremely poisonous. As few as two berries can induce vomiting, bloody diarrhea, and finally, cardiac arrest or respiratory paralysis. The genus name, *Actaea*, is derived from the Greek *aktaia*, meaning "elder tree," as the leaves are similar to elder leaves. The species name, *rubra*, is Latin for "red," a reference to the berries. There have been reports of children who have died as a result of eating the berries.

Globeflower
Trollius albiflorus (formerly *T. laxus*)

BUTTERCUP FAMILY

This plant grows from thick rootstock and fibrous roots and is found in moist meadows, along stream banks and in open, damp areas in the subalpine and alpine zones. The mostly basal leaves are shiny, bright green, palmately divided into five to seven parts, and deeply toothed. The stem leaves are few, alternate and short-stalked. The flowers are made up of five to ten white sepals (which may have a pinkish tint on the outside) that surround a central core filled with numerous dark yellow stamens.

There seems to be some confusion among the learned authorities as to the origin of the genus name, *Trollius*. The most likely resolution is that the genus name is a Latinized version of the Swiss-German common name, *trollblume*, which means "troll flower." The reference to the troll, a malevolent supernatural being, probably arises because this plant contains a poisonous alkaloid. Just prior to opening, and during inclement weather, the flower head appears round, thus the common name Globeflower. Globeflower might be confused with Mountain Marsh Marigold (*Caltha leptosepala*), shown on page 118, where they co-exist. The leaves of Mountain Marsh Marigold are heart-shaped, not oblong, and not divided into segments as are those of Globeflower.

Mountain Marsh Marigold
Caltha leptosepala

BUTTERCUP FAMILY

Virginia Skilton image

This plant lives in marshes, on stream banks, and in seeps in the subalpine and alpine zones. The leaves are mostly basal, simple, long-stemmed, oblong to blunt arrowhead-shaped, with wavy or round-toothed margins. The flowers are solitary on the end of the stem, and consist of 5 to 12 petal-like sepals that are white, tinged with blue on the back. The flower has a bright yellow centre, composed of numerous stamens and pistils.

The genus name, *Caltha*, is derived from the Greek *kalathos*, which means "goblet," most probably a reference to the shape of the open flower. The species name, *leptosepala*, is derived from the Greek *lepto*, which means "thin or narrow," and *sepala*, referring to the sepals. This plant contains glucosides, which are poisonous. The plant also goes by the locally common names of Elkslip and Elkslip Marshmarigold. Mountain Marsh Marigold might be confused with Globeflower (*Trollius albiflorus*), shown on page 117, which grows in similar habitat. The flowers are similar, but the leaves on Globeflower are deeply divided and sharply toothed.

Water Crowfoot (Water Buttercup)
Ranunculus aquatilis

BUTTERCUP FAMILY

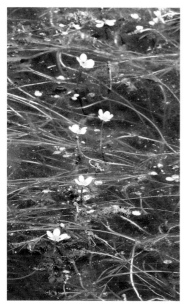 

This aquatic Buttercup lives in ponds, lakes, slow-moving streams, and ditches. The white flowers have five sepals, five to ten petals, and numerous pistils and stamens. The plant has two types of leaves. The submerged leaves are thread-like filaments that are matting, and the floating leaves are deeply cleft into three to five lobes. The flowers are flecked with gold at the base and buoyed above the water's surface on short stems. Yellow Water Crowfoot, which has yellow petals, is now considered to be in the same species. See photograph on the right above.

The origin of the genus name, *Ranunculus*, is discussed in the note on Creeping Buttercup (*R. repens*), shown on page 8. This plant can occur in abundance, and sometimes covers the surface of small ponds and slow-moving streams. Water Crowfoot is pollinated by insects. The common name, Crowfoot, may originate as a reference to the shape of the floating leaves.

Western Anemone (Chalice Flower)
Pulsatilla occidentalis (also *Anemone occidentalis*)

BUTTERCUP FAMILY

This plant is considered by many to be characteristic of wet alpine meadows and clearings. The large, creamy-white flowers bloom early in the spring, as the leaves are beginning to emerge. The entire plant is covered with hairs, which keep the plant protected in its cold habitat. Most of the leaves are basal, but there is a ring of feathery, grey-green stem leaves just below the flower. The flower is replaced by a clumped top of plumed seeds at the tip of the flowering stem. These seed clusters have been variously referred to as "mops," "shaggy heads," and "blond wigs," and give rise to another common name, Towhead Babies.

The common name, Chalice Flower, refers to the cup-shape inflorescence of the plant. A more recently coined name that has found some favour is Hippie on a Stick, a reference to the seed pod of the plant. The plant also goes by the locally common name Western Pasqueflower.

Western Clematis (White Virgin's Bower)
Clematis ligusticifolia

BUTTERCUP FAMILY

This plant is a climbing or trailing, woody vine that occurs in coulees, creek bottoms, and river valleys. It clings to and climbs over other plants by a twist or kink in its leaf stalks. The leaves are opposite and compound, with five to seven long-stalked leaflets. The flowers are white, and borne in dense clusters. The flowers are unisexual. The male flowers have many stamens but no pistils, while the female flowers have both pistils and sterile stamens.

The origin of the genus and common name is explained in the note on Blue Clematis (*C. occidentalis*), shown on page 73. The whole plant is toxic if ingested. Some Native peoples mashed the leaves and branches and used the juices as a headwash. Some also boiled the leaves and applied the decoction to boils and sores. Clematis also occurs in Yellow (*C. tangutica*), a naturalized variety. The plant often goes by the locally common names of Virgin's Bower and Traveller's Joy, both names arising because the plant creates bowers along trellises and fences, creating shelters and shady areas. The flowers of Yellow and Blue Clematis are quite different in appearance from Western Clematis. The flowers of these species resemble crepe paper.

Chocolate Tips
Lomatium dissectum

CARROT FAMILY

This large plant has several stout, smooth, hairless stems, and grows to over 1 m tall in dry, rocky places. The leaves are large (up to 30 cm), finely dissected and fern-like, and have a spicy aroma. The surface of the leaves has a covering of fine hairs, making it rough to the touch. The flowers are compound umbels of deep purplish-brown or yellow flowers sitting atop the ends of the stems. The fruits are elliptic seeds with flattened backs and corky, thick-winged margins.

The genus name, *Lomatium*, is derived from the Greek *loma*, meaning "a border," most probably a reference to the winged or ribbed fruit of most of the members of the genus. All members of the genus are edible. The specific name, *dissectum*, describes the finely dissected foliage. Meriwether Lewis collected a specimen of the plant in present-day Idaho in 1806 and labelled it "a great horse medicine among the natives." Another common name for the plant is Fern-Leaved Desert Parsley.

Cow Parsnip
Heracleum lanatum

CARROT FAMILY

A plant of shaded riverine habitat, stream banks, and moist open aspen woods, this plant can grow to over 2 m tall. The flowers are distinctive in large, compound, umbrella-shaped clusters (umbels) composed of numerous white flowers with white petals in fives. The leaves are compound in threes, usually very large, softly hairy, deeply lobed, and toothed.

Heracleum refers to Hercules, likely because of the plant's large size. Cow Parsnip is also locally known as Indian Celery and Indian Rhubarb. The roots were cooked and eaten by some Native peoples, though there are some sources that say they are poisonous. The Blackfoot roasted the young spring stalks and ate them. They also used the stalks in their Sun Dance ceremony. Caution should be taken to distinguish this plant from the violently poisonous Water Hemlock (*Cicuta maculata*), shown on page 128.

Large-Fruited Desert-Parsley
Lomatium macrocarpum

CARROT FAMILY

This low growing, stout perennial grows from an elongated taproot and puts up a stem that branches near the base and grows up to 50 cm tall in dry areas, open slopes, and gravelly sites. The leaves are all basal, hairy, clustered near the ground, greyish in colour, and finely dissected to resemble fern leaves in appearance. The flowers are white to purplish and occur in large umbrella-shaped clusters at the top of multiple stems. The fruits are long and smooth, with narrow wings.

The origin of the genus name, *Lomatium*, is discussed in the note on Chocolate Tips (*L. dissectum*), shown on page 122. The specific name, *macrocarpum*, means "with large fruits." Native peoples used the plant for food, usually digging up the taproots before the plant bloomed in the spring. The roots are said to have a peppery taste and were eaten raw or cooked. Other common names for the plant are Indian Carrot, Indian Sweet Potato, and Bigseed Biscuitroot.

Queen Anne's Lace
Daucus carota

CARROT FAMILY

This is an invasive weed imported from Eurasia, now common in disturbed ground, moist meadows, fields, and roadsides all over North America. It is a single-stemmed biennial that grows to 120 cm tall. The leaves are very finely dissected, like those of garden carrot plants. The inflorescence occurs as compound umbels in compact heads of hundreds of tiny yellow-white flowers atop the stem. The central floret in the umbel is often purple or pink. When the plant goes to seed, the outer, longer spokes of the umbel arch inward, forming a "bird's nest" effect.

The genus name, *Daucus*, is the Greek name for a similar Old World species. The species name, *carota*, is derived from the Greek *karoton*, which means "carrot." Indeed, this plant is also known as Wild Carrot. There are a number of explanations offered as to the origin of the common name Queen Anne's Lace. As an example, one explanation holds that the name refers to Queen Anne of England, who was an expert lace maker. The legend has it that the Queen, while making lace, pricked her finger with a needle and a drop of blood from the wound fell onto the lace, similar to the purple floret in the middle of the inflorescence.

Sharptooth Angelica (Lyall's Angelica)
Angelica arguta

CARROT FAMILY

This plant can grow to over 2 m tall in shaded riverine habitat, stream banks, and moist open woods. The numerous white flowers are arranged in compound umbels. The leaves are twice compound, with large leaflets that are sharply toothed, as is reflected in the common name for the plant. The lateral leaf veins are directed to the ends of the teeth on the leaf margin. The very poisonous Water Hemlock (*Cicuta maculata*), shown on page 128, has similar flowers, and should not be confused with Sharptooth Angelica. In Water Hemlock the leaf veins are directed to the notch between the teeth on the leaf margin.

The genus name, *Angelica*, is derived from the Latin *angelus*, meaning "an angel." There appear to be several schools of thought as to how this reference to angels arose. One account has it that a revelation was made by an angel to Matthaeus Sylvaticus, a 14th-century physician who compiled a dictionary of medical recipes of the beneficial medicinal properties of the plant. Another school of thought holds that the flower usually blooms at about the time of the feast of St. Michael the Archangel. The species name, *arguta*, is Latin meaning, among other things, "sharp" or "pungent." The other common name, Lyall's Angelica, is in honour of David Lyall, a Scottish botanist and geologist who collected specimens while working on the boundary survey between Canada and the United States in the 1880s. Angelicas are highly prized by herbalists for treating digestive disorders. Canby's Lovage (*Ligusticum canbyi*) has a similar flower and occurs in similar habitat and it may be confused with Sharptooth Angelica. That plant has compound leaves divided into three parts, then divided again into many smaller, deeply cleft segments.

Sweet Cicely
Osmorhiza berteroi (formerly *O. chilensis*)

CARROT FAMILY

This member of the Carrot Family prefers moist to wet, shady habitat, and grows up to 1 m tall. The leaves are twice divided into three parts, and are deeply cleft and toothed. The flowers are inconspicuous and occur in white to greenish compound, umbrella-shaped clusters. The fruits of the plants in this genus have short beaks that often cling to the fur of passing animals or the clothing of passing hikers.

The genus name, *Osmorhiza*, is derived from the Greek *osme*, meaning "scent," and *rhiza*, meaning "root," a reference to the sweet licorice odour given off by the plant's roots and fruits when they are crushed. Many Native peoples used the roots as food, and also for a variety of medicinal purposes. Some tribes held the plant sacred, and prohibited all but holy men from touching it. The plant is also known locally as Mountain Sweet Cicely.

Water Hemlock
Cicuta maculata (also *C. douglasii*)

CARROT FAMILY

This is a plant of marshes, river and stream banks and low, wet areas that produces several large umbrella-like clusters (compound umbels) of white flowers appearing at the top of a sturdy stalk. The leaves are alternate, with many bipinnate and tripinnate leaflets that are lance-shaped. The side veins in the leaflets end between the notched teeth on the leaflets, rather than at their points.

The genus name, *Cicuta*, is the Latin name of some poisonous members of the Carrot Family. While lovely to look at, with its umbrella-shaped clusters of flowers on sturdy stems, the Water Hemlock is considered to be perhaps the most poisonous plant in North America. All parts of the plant are poisonous, as testified to by several common names which include Children's Bane, Beaver Poison, and Death of Man. The toxin – cicutoxin – acts on the central nervous system and causes violent convulsions, followed by paralysis and respiratory failure. Some Native peoples used the powdered root as a poison on arrows. If you touch this plant or cut it with an implement for any reason, wash your hands and the implement immediately and thoroughly.

Arrow-Leaved Sweet Coltsfoot

Petasites sagittatus

COMPOSITE FAMILY

This plant occurs from low to subalpine elevations in wetlands, ditches, and slough margins, sometimes appearing in standing water. The basal leaves are large, long-stalked, triangular to heart-shaped, have toothed margins, and are densely white-woolly underneath. The flowering stems appear prior to the basal leaves. The stem does not have leaves, but does have some overlapping bracts. The flowers are a torch-like cluster of composite heads with glandular, woolly-hairy bases, sitting atop the stem. The flowers consist almost entirely of whitish disk flowers, sometimes with a few white ray flowers.

The genus name, *Petasites*, is derived from the Greek *petasos*, which means "broad-brimmed hat," a reference to the large leaves. Members of the genus have long been used in herbal medicine to treat coughs, asthma, and colic. The leaves were also used in poultices for wounds and inflammations. The leaves yield a yellowish-green dye. A similar species, Palmate Coltsfoot (*P. frigidus*), shown on page 133, appears in the same habitat but it has leaf blades that are palmately lobed into five to seven sharply toothed segments.

Daisy Fleabane
Erigeron compositus

COMPOSITE FAMILY

This daisy-like flower is one of several Fleabanes that occur in the region. The leaves of this species are almost all basal, and are deeply divided. The leaves and the flowering stems are sparsely covered with short, glandular hairs. The flowers appear solitary at the top of the stem, and they are typical of flowers in the Composite Family in that they have ray flowers surrounding disk flowers. The ray flowers are numerous, and may be white, pink, or mauve. The disk flowers are numerous and yellow. The involucral bracts are hairy and purplish at the tips.

The genus name, *Erigeron*, is derived from the Greek *eri*, which means "spring," and *geron*, which means "old man," a reference to the hairy-tufted fruits of plants in the genus, or perhaps to the overall hairiness of many species in the genus. The species name, *compositus*, means "well-arranged," probably in reference to the neat appearance of the inflorescence. The common name, Fleabane, arises because it was once thought that bundles of these flowers brought into the house would repel fleas. The plant also goes by the locally common names Cutleaf Fleabane and Cutleaf Daisy. Fleabanes and Asters are often confused. Fleabanes generally have narrower, more numerous ray florets than Asters. In addition, if you check the involucral bract – the small green cup under the flower – and see that all of the bracts are the same length, then you have a Fleabane. If some of the bracts are obviously shorter, you have an Aster.

Hooker's Thistle
Cirsium hookerianum

COMPOSITE FAMILY

This thistle can grow up to a metre tall, and is found in a variety of habitats, from valleys up to alpine elevations. The flower heads are white and the bracts surrounding the flowers point upward. The leaves, stems, and bracts are all covered with silky hairs. The leaves display a prominent midvein.

The origin of the genus name, *Cirsium*, is explained in the narrative on Bull Thistle (*C. vulgare*), shown on page 235. The species name, *hookerianum*, celebrates Sir William Hooker, a prestigious English botanist who wrote extensively on the subject and was a director of the Kew Herbarium and Botanical Garden in England in the mid-19th century. This plant was used as food by some Native peoples, eaten either raw or cooked.

Ox-Eye Daisy
Leucanthemum vulgare (also *Chrysanthemum leucanthemum*)

COMPOSITE FAMILY

An invasive Eurasian perennial from a well developed rhizome, this plant frequents low to middle elevations in moist to moderately dry sites such as roadsides, clearings, pastures, and disturbed areas. The flowers are solitary composite heads at the end of branches, with white ray flowers and yellow disk flowers. The basal leaves are broadly lance-shaped or narrowly spoon-shaped. The stem leaves are oblong and smaller.

Daisy is from the Anglo-Saxon *day's eye*, a reference to the fact that the English daisy closes at night and opens at sun-up. One of the most common and recognizable wildflowers in North America, the Ox-Eye Daisy is very prolific, and will overgrow large areas if not kept in check. A similar flower, Scentless Chamomile (*Matricaria perforata*) occurs in similar habitat and is often confused with Ox-Eye Daisy. To confirm the identity, closely inspect the leaves on the plant in issue. Scentless Chamomile has much thinner leaflets, and they are much more dissected than are those of Ox-Eye Daisy.

Palmate Coltsfoot
Petasites frigidus

COMPOSITE FAMILY

This perennial grows from a thick, creeping rhizome, putting up a white-hairy flowering stem that is up to 50 cm tall in wet to moist forests and wetlands, and along streams, rivers, and lakeshores at low to subalpine elevations. The stem appears before the leaves. The basal leaves are kidney-shaped to round, long-stalked, hairy, and palmately lobed into five to seven sharply toothed segments. The stem leaves are very much reduced to reddish bracts. The inflorescence occurs as a flat-topped cluster of composite heads at the top of the stem. The flower heads have white to pinkish ray and disk florets, or may appear with disk florets only. The flower heads have woolly-hairy bases.

The origin of the genus name, *Petasites*, is discussed in the note on Arrow-Leaved Sweet Coltsfoot (*P. sagittatus*), shown on page 129. The species name, *frigidus*, is Latin meaning "stiff," most probably a reference to the stiff hairs on the plant. The flowering stem of the plant arises from a different point on the rhizome than do the leaves, so their association may not be obvious. Native peoples used the plants as food, consuming the young leaves as pot herbs. They also burned he leaves of the plant, and used the ashes as a salt substitute. Members of the genus have long been used in herbal medicine to treat coughs, asthma, and colic. The leaves were also used in poultices for wounds and inflammations. The leaves yield a yellowish-green dye.

Pathfinder Plant (Trail Plant)
Adenocaulon bicolor

COMPOSITE FAMILY

This plant grows in shady and open woods at low to moderate elevations. The basal leaves are alternate, up to 30 cm long and 15 cm wide, triangular to heart-shaped, narrowly scalloped, and appear on slender stems that reach 1 m long. The leaves are green above and white woolly below. The flowering stem is solitary with many branches, and rises above the leaves. The inconspicuous white flowers occur in small heads in a panicle at the ends of the flowering stems. The flowers have disk florets only, no ray florets. The fruits are hooked achenes that cling to clothing or fur of passersby.

The genus name, *Adenocaulon*, is derived from the Greek *adenas*, which means "gland," and *kaulos*, which means "stem," a reference to the glandular hairs on the stems of the plant. The species name refers to the distinctive two colours of the opposite leaf surfaces. The common names originate from this distinctive feature. When a hiker or other stroller moves through the plants, the leaves invert, showing the silvery white undersides. If the hiker looks back on the route taken, the path is obvious by the line of white leaves showing the trail.

Pearly Everlasting
Anaphalis margaritacea

COMPOSITE FAMILY

This plant grows in gravelly open woods and subalpine meadows in the mountains. There are numerous stem leaves, alternately attached directly to the stem. The leaves are lance-shaped and light green, with very soft fuzzy hairs. The white flowers occur in a dense, rounded terminal cluster. The male and female flowers occur on separate plants. The flowers have only disk flowers, no ray flowers, and often have a brown spot at the base.

The genus name, *Anaphalis*, is thought to be an invention of Carolus Linnaeus, relating this genus to a somewhat related genus, *Gnaphalium*, which name was, in turn, derived from the Greek *knaphalon*, which means a "tuft of wool." It could be said that the flowers of this species resemble tufts of wool. The common name, Pearly Everlasting, comes from the fact that the dried flowers resemble pearls and often last for a long time. The species name, *margaritacea*, means "of pearls," and is undoubtedly a reference to the shape of the flowers. The plant resembles Pussytoes (*Antennaria* spp.) but has more leaves, and the leaves are not reduced in size from the base to the top of the plant as they are in most Pussytoes.

Yarrow
Achillea millefolium

COMPOSITE FAMILY

This is a plant of dry to moist grasslands, open riverine forests, aspen woods, and disturbed areas. The individual white flower heads appear in a dense, flat-topped or rounded terminal cluster. The ray florets are white to cream-coloured (sometimes pink), and the central disk florets are straw-coloured. The leaves are woolly, greyish to blue-green, and finely divided, almost appearing to be a fern. Yarrow can occur in large colonies.

The common name is derived from the name of a Scottish parish. The genus name, *Achillea*, is in honour of Achilles, the Greek warrior with the vulnerable heel, who was said to have made an ointment from this plant to heal the wounds of his soldiers during the siege of Troy. The species name, *millefolium*, means "thousand leaves," in reference to the many finely divided leaf segments. Yarrow contains an alkaloid called achillein that reduces the clotting time of blood. It appears a number of Native peoples were aware of this characteristic of the plant, and made a mash of the crushed leaves to wrap around wounds.

Northern Black Currant (Skunk Currant)
Ribes hudsonianum

CURRANT FAMILY

This plant is an erect deciduous shrub, growing up to 2 m tall at low to subalpine elevations in moist to wet forests. The plant does not have thorns, but does have yellow resin glands dotting its smooth bark. The leaves are alternate and maple-leaf-shaped, with three to five rounded lobes. The flowers are white, saucer-shaped, and occur in spreading to erect clusters. The flowers have a strong smell that some people find objectionable. The fruits are black, speckled with resin dots, and are said to have a particularly bitter taste.

The origin of the genus name, *Ribes*, is discussed in the note on Black Gooseberry (*R. lacustre*), shown on page 242. The specific name, *hudsonianum*, means "of or around Hudson's Bay," a reference to where the plant was first collected for scientific description. Berries of all Currants are high in pectin, and can make excellent jams and jellies, though the raw berries are often insipid.

Sticky Currant
Ribes viscosissimum

CURRANT FAMILY

This plant is a shrub that grows up to 2 m high in damp woods and openings, from valleys to subalpine elevations. It does not have prickles. The flowers are bell-shaped, yellowish-white, and often tinged in pink. The flowers and leaves are covered in glandular hairs that are sticky to the touch. The fruits are blue-black, sticky, and not considered edible.

The origin of the genus name, *Ribes*, is discussed in the note on Black Gooseberry (*R. lacustre*), shown on page 242. The species name, *viscosissimum*, is the superlative degree of the Latin adjective *viscosus*, meaning "sticky" or "viscid." The first known botanical specimen was collected by Meriwether Lewis in present-day Idaho in 1806. Lewis's note on the plant in his journal says that the fruit is "indifferent & gummy."

Bunchberry (Dwarf Dogwood)
Cornus canadensis

DOGWOOD FAMILY

This is a plant of moist coniferous woods, often found on rotting logs and stumps. The flowers are clusters of inconspicuous greenish-white flowers set among four white, petal-like, showy bracts. The leaves are in a terminal whorl of four to seven, all prominently veined. The leaves are dark green above and lighter underneath. The fruits are bright red berries.

The genus name, *Cornus*, is Latin for "horn" or "antler," possibly a reference to the hard wood of some members of this genus. Another school of thought is that the inflorescence of the plant bears a resemblance to the cornice piece, a knob on cylinders used for rolling up manuscripts. *Canadensis* is a reference to Canada, this plant being widely distributed across the country in the boreal forests. Bunchberry's common name is probably derived from the fact that the fruits are all bunched together in a terminal cluster. A Nootka legend has it that the Bunchberry arose from the blood of a woman marooned in a cedar tree by her jealous husband. The plant is reported to have an explosive pollination mechanism wherein the petals of the mature but unopened flower buds suddenly reflex and the anthers spring out, casting pollen loads into the air. When an insect brushes against the tiny bristle at the end of one petal, it triggers this explosion.

Red-Osier Dogwood
Cornus stolonifera

DOGWOOD FAMILY

This willow-like shrub that grows up to 3 m high, often forming impenetrable thickets along streams and in moist forests. The reddish bark is quite distinctive, and it becomes even redder with the advent of frosts. The leaves are heavily veined, dark green above and pale underneath. The flowers are small, greenish-white, and occur in a flat-topped cluster at the terminal ends of stems. The fruits are small white berries, appearing in clumps.

The origin of the genus name, *Cornus*, is discussed in the note on Bunchberry (*C. canadensis*), shown on page 139. The common name, Osier, appears to be from the Old French *osiere*, meaning "that which grows in an osier-bed (streambed)." Native peoples used the branches of the plant to fashion fish traps, poles, and salmon stretchers. This plant is extremely important winter browse for moose.

140

Eyebright
Euphrasia nemorosa

FIGWORT FAMILY

These small, beautiful plants grow from a taproot that puts up slender, hairy, erect, sometimes branching stems that may reach 40 cm tall in moist woods at moderate to high elevations. The leaves are sessile (stalkless), egg-shaped to somewhat circular, sparsely hairy, glandular, and have decidedly toothed margins. The upper leaves are reduced in size, and the white flowers appear in the axils. The flowers are two-lipped, with the upper lip being two-lobed and concave, and the lower lip having three spreading, notched lobes. There is purple pencilling on the lips and a yellow spot on the lower lip.

The genus name, *Euphrasia*, is derived from the Greek *euphrosyne*, which means "gladness," though the reference is lost. The specific name, *nemorosa*, means "well-wooded," "full of foliage," presumably a reference to the preferred habitat. The plant has long been used medicinally. It has historically been mixed with other herbs to treat conjunctivitis and other inflammations of the eye, as well as used as an eyewash. Presumably that is the source of the common name. These small flowers deserve close attention when encountered, in order to see the fine details of their construction.

Sickletop Lousewort (Parrot's Beak)
Pedicularis racemosa

FIGWORT FAMILY

This lovely plant favours upper montane and subalpine environments. The white flower has a very distinctive shape that deserves close examination to appreciate its intricacy. The flowers appear along a purplish-coloured stem that grows up to 35 cm tall. The leaves are simple, lance-shaped to linear, and have distinctive fine, sharp teeth on the margins.

The origin of the genus name, *Pedicularis*, is explained in the narrative on Bracted Lousewort (*P. bracteosa*), shown on page 32. Sickletop Lousewort takes its common name from the long, slender downward turned beak on the upper lip of the petals. Another common name, Parrot's Beak, is a reference to the shape of the flowers. Some people call the plant Leafy Lousewort. Another similar species with creamy-white flowers occurs in the region, the Contorted Lousewort (*P. contorta*), but it usually is found at higher elevations.

White Geranium
Geranium richardsonii

GERANIUM FAMILY

A plant of moist grasslands, open woods, and thickets, this plant is very similar to Sticky Purple Geranium (*G. viscosissimum*), shown on page 87, except it has white to pinkish flowers with purple veins. The petals have long hairs at the base. The leaves are not sticky, and are hairy only along the veins of the lower sides of the leaves. The fruits are like those of the Sticky Purple Geranium, that is, capsules with long beaks, shaped like a crane's or stork's bill.

The origin of the genus name, *Geranium*, is discussed in the note on Sticky Purple Geranium. The species name, *richardsonii*, honours Sir John Richardson, a 19th-century Scottish botanist assigned to Sir John Franklin's expedition to the Arctic in search of the Northwest Passage. The fruit capsules are said to open explosively, with the beak splitting lengthwise from the bottom and catapulting the seeds away from the parent plant. White Geraniums seem to prefer partially shaded locations that are rich in humus.

Devil's Club
Oplopanax horridus

GINSENG FAMILY

If there were a contest for the meanest plant in the woods, this one would almost certainly qualify. Devil's Club is aptly named. It has club-shaped woody stems that grow to over 2 m tall, and the stems are covered in stiff, sharp spines. The leaves are large, shaped like very large maple leaves, with sharp spines on their veins and leaf stalks, and sharp teeth on their margins. The flowers are small, white, and globe-shaped, and are arranged along a central flower stalk up to 25 cm long. The fruits are a mass of shiny red berries.

The genus name, *Oplopanax*, is derived from the Greek *hoplon*, meaning "weapon." The species name, *horridus*, comes from the same root as "horrible." The spines of the plant easily break off in skin, and the punctures occasioned will quickly become sore and inflamed. In spite of all this, the plant is quite handsome and regal. It also has a number of medicinal properties, and has been used by Native peoples and herbalists to treat such diverse ailments as arthritis, diabetes, cataracts, and indigestion. It is recommended that this plant be given a good inspection, but do not get too close.

Wild Sarsaparilla
Aralia nudicaulis

GINSENG FAMILY

This plant prefers the dark woods of the moist montane forests. The leaves are up to 50 cm long, arising singly from an underground stem. Each leaf has a long bare stalk that terminates in three to five leaflets each. The leaflets are up to 15 cm long, and are sharply toothed and pointed at the ends. The flowers arise from a short stem near ground level, well below the spreading leaflets. The flowers are tiny, whitish-green, and arranged in three round shaped umbels.

The genus name, *Aralia*, is the Latinized form of the French *aralie*, the Québec *habitant* name for the plant. The species name, *nudicaulis*, means "bare stem," a reference to the leafless flower stalk. The plant was used as a stimulant in sweat lodges by some Native peoples, and was also used in a variety of other medicinal ways.

Fringed Grass-of-Parnassus
Parnassia fimbriata

GRASS-OF-PARNASSUS FAMILY

These plants abound in riverine habitat, pond edges, and boggy places from montane to the subalpine zone. The white flowers are very delicate-looking. The flowers appear as singles on a slender stem, with five white petals and greenish or yellowish veins. The lower edges of the petals are fringed with hairs. Alternating fertile and sterile stamens are characteristic of this genus. The leaves are mostly basal and broadly kidney-shaped. A single leaf clasps the flowering stem about halfway up.

The name of this plant seems to present some confusion. One school of thought is that the genus name, *Parnassia*, is from Mount Parnassus in Greece, said to be a favourite retreat of the god Apollo. Another school of thought holds that the name comes from a description of the plant written in the 1st century by Dioscorides, a military physician for the Roman emperor Nero. When the description was translated, "grass" was included in the translation, and it stuck. There is no doubt that this plant is not even remotely grass-like. A similar species, Northern Grass-of-Parnassus (*P. palustris*) occurs in the similar habitat, but it does not have the fringed margins of Fringed Grass-of-Parnassus.

Greenish-Flowered Wintergreen (Green Wintergreen)
Pyrola chlorantha (also *P. virens*)

HEATH FAMILY

This is an erect perennial that inhabits moist to dry coniferous and mixed forests, and riverine environments, from the montane to the subalpine zones. The flowers have five greenish-white, waxy petals, and a long style attached to a prominent ovary. The flowers have a bell shape and are distributed on short stalks up the main stem. The leaves are basal, in a rosette. The leaves have a leathery appearance and are shiny, rounded, and dark green.

The genus name, *Pyrola*, is derived from Latin *pyrus*, which means "a pear," probably a reference to the leaves being pear-shaped. Wintergreen leaves contain acids that are effective in treating skin irritations. Mashed leaves of *Pyrola* species have traditionally been used by herbalists in skin salves, and poultices for snake and insect bites. They are called wintergreen, not because of the taste, but because the leaves remain green during the winter. Like orchids, these plants require a specific fungus in the soil to grow successfully, and transplantation should not be attempted. Another species of *Pyrola*, Pink Wintergreen, (*P. asarifolia*), shown on page 260, is similar in shape and occurs in similar habitat, but has pink flowers.

Indian Pipe (Ghost Plant)
Monotropa uniflora

HEATH FAMILY

This unique and unusual plant grows either solitary or in clumps from a dense root system, and occurs in moist, shaded woods in rich soil. It is fairly rare and is said to appear almost overnight, like a mushroom. Instead of leaves, it has colourless scales. The flowers are white to cream-coloured, nodding on stems up to 20 cm tall and shaped like a smoking pipe stuck into the ground by its stem. The flowers darken to black with age, and turn upward at the top of the stem. Stems from the previous year's growth may persist.

The genus name, *Monotropa*, is derived from the Greek *monos*, meaning "single," and *tropos*, meaning "direction," a reference to the flowers being turned to one side. This plant contains no chlorophyll and is saprophytic, meaning it obtains its nutrients from dead and decaying plant or animal matter. Native peoples used the plant for a number of medicinal purposes. Other common names applied to the plant are Ghost Flower, Corpse Plant, and Ice Plant. Another member of the genus, Pine-Sap (*M. hypopithys*) exists in similar habitat, but it is rarer yet. It has numerous urn-shaped, light brown to cream-coloured flowers on its stem.

Labrador Tea
Ledum groenlandicum

HEATH FAMILY

This evergreen, much-branched shrub is widespread in low to subalpine elevations in peaty wetlands and moist coniferous forests. The flowers are white and numerous, with five to ten protruding stamens in umbrella-like clusters at the ends of branches. The leaves are alternate and narrow, with edges rolled under. They are deep green and leathery on top, with dense rusty hairs underneath.

The genus name, *Ledum*, is derived from the Greek *ledon*, which means "mastic," the Greek name for an Old World plant whose foliage resembles that of this species. The leaves, used fresh or dried, can be brewed into an aromatic tea, but should be used in moderation to avoid drowsiness. Excessive doses are reported to act as a strong diuretic. The aromatic leaves were used in barns to drive away mice, and in houses to keep away fleas.

Lingonberry
Vaccinium vitis-idaea

HEATH FAMILY

Virginia Skilton image

This plant is a creeping or trailing, many-branched, mat-forming evergreen dwarf shrub that grows up to 10–20 cm tall in moist places, on open slopes, and on raised areas in bogs, mostly in the northern part of the region. The small leaves are alternate, leathery, and have rolled edges with black dots on the undersides. The flowers are whitish to light pink and urn-shaped, occurring in short clusters at the branch ends. The fruits are red berries that are 5–10 mm in diameter.

The genus name, *Vaccinium*, is the Latin name for Blueberry. The species name, *vitis-idaea*, is derived from the Latin *vitis*, which means "grape vine," and Idaea, who was a nymph in Greek mythology. Other locally common names are Cowberry, Foxberry, and Mountain Cranberry. Low-Bush Cranberry (*Viburnum edule*), shown on page 158, also appears in the region, but it is a member of the Honeysuckle Family and is a substantially different plant. There is in the region another plant also known as Bog Cranberry (*V. oxycoccos*), shown on page 255. It has pink nodding flowers, with the petals curved backward, similar in shape to Shooting Star (*Dodecatheon pulchellum*), shown on page 101.

One-Sided Wintergreen
Pyrola secunda (also *Orthilia secunda*)

HEATH FAMILY

This small forest dweller grows to 5–15 cm tall at low to subalpine elevations in dry to moist coniferous or mixed woods and clearings. The white to yellowish-green flowers lie on one side of the arching stalk, arranged in a raceme of six to ten flowers, sometimes more. The flowers resemble small street lights strung along a curving pole. The straight style sticks out beyond the petals, with a flat, five-lobed stigma. The leaves are basal, egg-shaped, and finely toothed at the margins.

Some taxonomists include One-Sided Wintergreen in the *Pyrola* genus, while others put it in genus *Orthilia*. The origin of the genus name, *Pyrola*, is explained in the note on Greenish-Flowered Wintergreen (*P. chlorantha*), shown on page 147. *Orthilia* is derived from the Greek *orthos*, meaning "straight," most probably a reference to the straight style. The species name, *secunda*, is Latin meaning "next" or "following," a reference to the flowers which follow each other on the same side of the stem. The plant also goes by the aptly descriptive, locally common name Sidebells Wintergreen. Once seen, this delightful little flower is unmistakable in the woods.

Painted Pyrola (White-Veined Wintergreen)
Pyrola picta

HEATH FAMILY

This erect perennial inhabits moist coniferous and mixed forests. The flowers are similar to Greenish-Flowered Wintergreen (*P. chlorantha*), shown on page 147 – bell shaped, waxy and distributed along the main stalk – but the leaf of this plant is the distinguishing feature. The leaves of Painted Pyrola are thick, glossy, and green, with extraordinarily beautiful white mottling along the veins of the upper surface. This mottling gives the plant its other common name, White-Veined Wintergreen. The pale areas on the leaf's surface are caused by a lack of chlorophyll, which indicates the partially parasitic nature of the plant.

The origin of the genus name, *Pyrola*, is discussed in the note on Greenish-Flowered Wintergreen. The species name, *picta*, means "painted" or "brightly coloured," no doubt a reference to the leaves. The plant also goes by the locally common name Nootka Wintergreen, a reference to Nootka Sound or Nootka Island, British Columbia, where the plant apparently was first discovered. Wintergreen leaves contain acids which are effective in treating skin irritations. Like orchids, these plants require a specific fungus in the soil to grow successfully and transplantation should not be attempted. Another species of *Pyrola*, Pink Wintergreen, (*P. asarifolia*), shown on page 260, is similar in shape and occurs in similar habitat, but has pink flowers.

Single Delight
Moneses uniflora (also *Pyrola uniflora*)

HEATH FAMILY

This delightful little forest dweller is also known as One-Flowered Winter-green, and it inhabits damp forests, usually on rotting wood. The plant is quite tiny, standing only 15 cm tall, and the single white flower, open and nodding at the top of the stem, is less than 5 cm in diameter. The flower looks like a small white umbrella, offering shade. The leaves are basal, oval, and evergreen, attached to the base of the stem. The style is prominent and tipped with a five-lobed stigma that almost looks like a mechanical part of some kind.

The genus name, *Moneses*, is derived from the Greek *monos*, meaning "solitary," and *hesia*, meaning "delight," a reference to the delightful single flower. Other common names include Wood Nymph and Shy Maiden. In Greek mythology, nymphs were nature goddesses, beautiful maidens living in rivers, woods, and mountains, and once you see this diminutive flower, the common names seem completely appropriate.

Western Tea-Berry
Gaultheria ovatifolia

HEATH FAMILY

Virginia Skilton images

This evergreen shrub is sprawling and ground-hugging, only 5 cm tall, and occurs in a variety of habitat from open ponderosa pine forests, to cold bogs, to subalpine slopes. The stems on the plant are very thin, brownish, and hairy. The leaves are glossy, alternate, egg- to heart-shaped with saw-toothed margins, and grow up to 4 cm long. The white/cream or pink flowers are small, bell- or urn-shaped, nodding, and hairy. They occur singly in the axils of the leaves.

The genus name, *Gaultheria*, honours Dr. Jean-François Gaultier, an 18th-century French-Canadian physician and naturalist. The species name, *ovatifolia*, is a reference to the shape of the leaves of the plant. The plant goes by several locally common names, including Oregon Spicy Wintergreen, Oregon Wintergreen, Mountain Checkerberry, and Western Wintergreen. Creeping Snowberry (*G. hispidula*) is a related plant that grows in the region. It is a creeping, matted evergreen that has pinkish, bell-shaped flowers, but its fruits are white, juicy, edible berries.

White Heather (White Mountain Heather)
Cassiope mertensiana

HEATH FAMILY

This matting plant occurs in the subalpine and alpine zones. The flowers are white, bell-shaped and nodding at the end of the stems. The leaves are opposite, evergreen, and pressed so closely to the stems that the stems are all but hidden. The foliage forms large, low mats on the ground.

The genus name, *Cassiope,* is from Greek mythology. Cassiopeia was the wife of Cepheus, the King of the Ethiopians. She was vain and boastful, claiming that her beauty exceeded that of the sea nymphs. This claim offended and angered the sea nymphs, and they prevailed upon Poseidon, the god of the sea, to send a sea monster to punish Cassiopcia by ravaging the land. In order to save the kingdom, the Ethiopians offered Cassiopeia's daughter, Andromeda, as a sacrifice, chaining her to a rock. Perseus, the Greek hero who slew the Gorgon Medusa, intervened at the last minute to free Andromeda and slay the monster. In astronomy, the constellation Perseus stands between Cassiopeia and Andromeda, still defending her today. While interesting, what all that has to do with this flower is a mystery. The species name, *mertensiana,* honours F.C. Mertens, an early German botanist. In fact, White Mountain Heather is not a heather at all, but a heath.

White Rhododendron
Rhododendron albiflorum

HEATH FAMILY

This is an erect and spreading deciduous shrub that grows up to 2 m tall and inhabits cool, damp woods, often establishing dense communities under the conifer canopy. The leaves are oblong to lance-shaped, and are covered with fine rusty-coloured hairs. The leaves turn to beautiful shades of crimson and orange in the fall. The flowers are large (up to 3 cm across), white, and cup-shaped, and are borne singly or in small clusters around the stem of the previous year's growth. The petals are joined to each other for about half of their length, and there are 10 stamens visible inside the flower. The flowers are deciduous, and fall off of the plant as a whole, often littering the forest floor with what appear to be intact flowers.

The genus name, *Rhododendron*, is derived from the Greek *rhodon*, meaning "rose," and *dendron*, meaning "tree." The species name, *albiflorum*, is Latin meaning "white-flowered." This plant is often referred to as Mountain Misery because it grows in dense communities, with branches trailing downhill, making it difficult for hikers to move through it. The plant also has the locally common name Cascade Azalea. All parts of the plant contain poisonous alkaloids that are toxic to humans and livestock.

Blue Elderberry
Sambucus cerulea

HONEYSUCKLE FAMILY

This is a deciduous shrub that grows up to 4 m tall on streambanks and in open forests in valleys and up mountain slopes. The opposite, branching stems of the plant are woody, stout and filled with pith in the centre. The leaves are pinnately compound, with five to nine leaflets that are up to 15 cm long. The flowers are white to creamy, and occur in large flat-topped clusters at the summit of the branches. The fruits are waxy, pale powdery blue berries that appear in the late summer.

The genus name, *Sambucus*, is from the Greek *sambuke*, a musical instrument made from elderwood. The fruits of this plant have long been used as food. Wine and jellies can be produced from the berries. Bears seem quite partial to the fruits. The branches of the plant have been hollowed out to make whistles, drinking straws, pipe stems and blowguns, but that practice is discouraged because the branches of the plant contain glycosides and are poisonous. The common name Elder is said to be derived from the Anglo-Saxon *aeld*, which means "to kindle," a reference to the hollow stems of the plant being used to blow on tinder to start a fire. Two other Elderberries occur in the region: Black Elderberry (*S. racemosa* var. *melanocarpa*), which has black fruits, and Red Elderberry (*S. racemosa* var. *arborescens*), which has red fruits.

Low-Bush Cranberry (Mooseberry)
Viburnum edule

HONEYSUCKLE FAMILY

This plant is a sprawling deciduous shrub that grows up to 2 m tall, from low to subalpine elevations in moist to wet forests, along streams, and in boggy areas. The leaves are opposite, sharply toothed, and maple-leaf shaped with three lobes. The tiny, white, five-parted flowers appear in flat-topped showy clusters between leaves along the stem. The fruits are clusters of red or orange berries that contain a large, flattened stone. The fruits remain on the plant after the leaves fall, and the over-ripe berries and decaying leaves often produce a musty odour in the woods near the plants.

The genus name, *Viburnum,* is the classical Latin for an Old World member of the genus. The species name, *edule,* means "edible," and refers to the fruits of the plant. The fruits are favoured by birds. The fruits were used extensively by Native peoples as food, and other parts of the plant were used medicinally. In the fall the leaves of this plant turn beautiful crimson and purple colours. Two other locally common names for the plant are Mooseberry and Squash-berry. Some confusion can arise because of the existence of a plant called a High-Bush Cranberry (*V. trilobum*), which occurs in similar habitat. That plant is a larger bush – almost a small tree – with similar flowers and fruits. Neither the Low-Bush or the High-Bush are truly Cranberries, which are members of the Heath Family.

Red Twinberry (Utah Honeysuckle)
Lonicera utahensis

HONEYSUCKLE FAMILY

This erect deciduous shrub grows up to 2 m tall at low to subalpine elevations in moist to wet forest openings and clearings in the southern portion of the region. The leaves are opposite, elliptical to oblong, with smooth edges and blunt tips. The creamy-white flowers are trumpet-shaped and appear in pairs on a single stalk from the leaf axils. The fruits are red berries that are joined at the base.

The origin of the genus name, *Lonicera*, is discussed in the note on Black Twinberry (*L. involucrata*), shown on page 39. The specific name, *utahensis*, refers to the State of Utah, where the first specimen of the plant was collected for scientific description. Some Native peoples ate the berries, which were said to be a good emergency source of water because they are so juicy. The flowers are frequented by hummingbirds, which are said to use the flower extensively for food. The plant is also known as Utah Honeysuckle.

Mock Orange
Philadelphus lewisii

HYDRANGEA FAMILY

This stiff and densely branched, erect deciduous shrub grows up to 3 m tall in thickets, on rocky hillsides, in crevices and along streams from valley to subalpine elevations. The leaves occur in opposite pairs on the stems, and the bark of the shrub is reddish-brown to grey. The plant flowers in the late spring, producing lots of white flowers, which have four oblong white petals, four styles and many stamens. The flower emits a sweet, orange-blossom aroma. The fruits are hard capsules that overwinter on the shrub.

There is some disagreement among the authorities as to how this plant got its scientific name. One school of thought has it that the genus name, *Philadelphus*, has its origins in the Greek *philos*, which means "friend," and *adelphos*, meaning "brother," thus, approximately, "brotherly love," as in the motto of the city of Philadelphia, Pennsylvania. The other school of thought attributes the genus name to a commemoration of the Pharaoh Ptolemy II Philadelphus. The species name honours Meriwether Lewis, who first collected a specimen of the plant in 1806 along the Clearwater River in present-day Idaho. Mock Orange is the floral emblem of the State of Idaho. The plant often goes by the locally common name of Syringa, which is puzzling because that name is the genus name for lilacs, which are a totally unrelated plant.

Beargrass
Xerophyllum tenax

LILY FAMILY

These impressive plants grow in peaty soil or clay in open woods and clearings from middle elevations to the subalpine. The plant has a basal clump of dense, sharp, evergreen leaves, from which rises an impressive stem up to 1.5 m tall. The flowers are a torch-shaped cluster of hundreds of small, white miniature lilies, which bloom first from the bottom of the cluster, and then work their way upward. Individual plants may be sterile for several years, producing flowers only one to three times in a decade.

Some authorities attribute the common name Beargrass to the fact that bears have been reported to eat the leaves in the spring, but my research has led me to a different conclusion. The plant was first collected for science by Meriwether Lewis in 1806 in present-day Idaho. At the time of the collection, Lewis believed the plant to be a kind of Yucca (*Yucca glauca*), a plant that was known to Lewis by one of its common names, "bear grass." Beargrass has some resemblance to Yucca, but Yucca grows in more arid environments at lower elevations. Even though Lewis was mistaken about this plant being a type of Yucca, the name Beargrass stuck. Native peoples are reported to have used the leaves for weaving exquisite baskets, capes, and hats. Indeed, Indian Basket Grass is a locally common name for the plant. Various wild animals feed on various parts of the plant. The plant is said to be poisonous to humans if ingested.

Bronzebells
Stenanthium occidentale

LILY FAMILY

This lily of moist woods, stream banks, meadows, and slopes has grass-like leaves that emerge from an onion-like bulb. The bell-shaped flowers are greenish-white, flecked with purple, and have six sharply pointed tips that twist backward, exposing the interior of the blossom. Ten or more graceful and fragrant flowers are hung along the length of the stem, drooping down.

The genus name, *Stenanthium*, is derived from the Greek *stenos*, meaning "narrow," and *anthos*, meaning "flower." The appropriateness of this name will be testified to by any photographer who has tried to photograph this species in even a slight breeze. The species name, *occidentale*, means "western." Without question, this flower is extraordinarily attractive in its detail. Some authorities say the plant is poisonous; others say it is not. Apparently some Native peoples believed it to be poisonous. The plant also goes by the locally common names Mountain Bells and Western Mountainbells.

Clasping-Leaved Twisted-Stalk
Streptopus amplexifolius

LILY FAMILY

This plant grows in moist, shaded forests and has a widely branching zigzag stem with numerous sharp-pointed, parallel-veined leaves that encircle the stem at each angular bend. The plant varies in height from 30–100 cm. The glossy leaves often conceal the small, pale white or greenish flowers that dangle on curving, thread-like stalks from the axil of each of the upper leaves. In fact, one can walk by the plant without noticing the flowers hiding under the leaves. The flowers have strongly reflexed petals and sepals, and appear to be hanging on the plant like small spiders dangling on fine webs. The fruits of the plant are very handsome, orangish-red, oval berries.

The genus name, *Streptopus*, is derived from the Greek *streptos*, meaning "twisted," and *pous*, meaning "foot," referring to the twisted flower stalks. The species name, *amplexifolius*, is derived from the Latin *amplexor*, meaning "to surround," and *folius*, meaning "a leaf." Two other members of the genus occur in the region. Rosy Twisted Stalk (*S. roseus*) is a smaller plant with a stem that is unbranched and not conspicuously bent, and has rose-coloured bell-shaped flowers with white tips. Small Twisted Stalk (*S. streptopoides*) is smaller yet, has unbranched stems, and rose to purplish flowers that are saucer-shaped with the petal tips curled back.

Death Camas (Meadow Death Camas)
Zigadenus venenosus

LILY FAMILY

This plant of moist grasslands, grassy slopes, and open woods grows from an onion-like bulb that has no oniony smell. The leaves are mainly basal and resemble grass, with prominent midveins. The greenish-white, foul-smelling flowers appear in tight clusters atop an erect stem, each flower having three virtually identical petals and sepals. There are yellowish-green, V-shaped glands (nectaries) near the base of the petals and sepals.

The genus name, *Zigadenus*, is derived from the Greek *zygos*, meaning "yoke," and *adenas*, meaning "gland," a reference to the shape of the nectary at the base of each petal and sepal. The species name, *venenosus*, is Latin for "very poisonous." Death Camas contains poisonous alkaloids, and is probably even more toxic than its close relative, White Camas (*Z. elegans*), shown on page 173, which appears usually at higher elevations and blooms later. These plants have been responsible for killing many people and animals. When the flowers are absent, Death Camas and White Camas are difficult to distinguish from Early Camas (*Camassia quamash*), shown on page 91, the bulb of which was commonly used as food by Native peoples and early settlers. Failure to make this distinction was deadly.

Fairybells
Prosartes hookeri (formerly *Disporum hookeri*)

LILY FAMILY

A plant of moist shaded woods, stream banks, and riverine environments, this delightful flower blooms in early summer. The flowers have six tepals, and are bell-shaped, creamy white, and occur in drooping pairs at the end of branches. The leaves of the plant are generally lance-shaped with parallel veins and pointed ends. The fruits are reddish-orange egg-shaped berries, occurring in pairs.

While once in the genus *Disporum*, North American members of the genus were recently moved to the genus *Prosartes*, leaving only Eastern Asian species in the former genus. The genus name, *Prosartes*, is derived from the Greek *prosartes*, which means "attached," a reference to the manner in which the fruits are attached. The species name, *hookeri*, honours Joseph Dalton Hooker, who is considered by many to be the most important botanist of the 19th century. The fruits of Fairybells are edible, but said to be bland. They are a favoured food of many rodents and birds. The plant also goes by the locally common name Oregon Drops of Gold.

False Solomon's-Seal
Maianthemum racemosum (formerly *Smilacina racemosa*)

LILY FAMILY

A lily of moist woods, rivers and stream banks, thickets, and meadows, that can grow up to half a metre tall. The flowers are small and white, arranged in a branching panicle that is upright at the end of the stem. The leaves are broadly lance-shaped, numerous and alternate, gradually tapering to a pointed tip, with prominent parallel veining, sometimes folded at the midline. The fruit is a red berry flecked with maroon.

This plant was formerly in the genus *Smilacina*, but has now been moved to the genus *Maianthemum* as a result of molecular data establishing similarity to that different genus. *Maianthemum* is Latin for "May flower." The species name, *racemosum*, indicates that the plant has a raceme arrangement for the flowers. This name is somewhat confusing in that a raceme is an unbranched cluster of flowers on a common stalk. The flower arrangement on this plant is more precisely referred to as a panicle – a branched flower cluster that blooms from the bottom up. A very similar plant lives in the same habitat – the Star-Flowered Solomon's-Seal (*M. stellatum*), shown on page 169 – but it has significantly fewer flowers, which are shaped like six-sided stars.

Indian Hellebore (False Hellebore)
Veratrum viride

LILY FAMILY

This is a tall, stout, often fuzzy-haired perennial with many leaves that inhabits moist forests, thickets, bogs, wet meadows and avalanche chutes. The greenish flowers are somewhat inconspicuous and occur in long, open, drooping clusters along a substantial stalk that arises from the centre of the generally basal leaves. The stamens are yellow-tipped. Perhaps the most distinctive feature of this robust plant is the leaves. They are large, dull green, with long, closed sheaths at the base. Each leaf is broadly elliptic with a pointed tip, and has a prominently veined or ribbed smooth surface above and a hairy underside. The basal leaves appear well before the flowers, and seem to whirl up from the earth, dwarfing all other plants around them.

This plant is also known as Green False Hellebore, a reference apparently to the genus name, *Veratrum*, being used in ancient times to apply to a true hellebore, which was a member of the Helleborus Family. The genus name is derived from the Latin words *verus*, meaning "true," and *atrum*, meaning "black," a reference to the black roots of the true hellebore. The species name, *viride*, means "green." This plant contains very toxic alkaloids which can cause symptoms similar to heart attacks. People have died from eating it, and, indeed, the Blackfoot are said to have used the plant to commit suicide. The plant is most dangerous early in the growing season, and is said to have caused accidental poisonings among cattle and sheep. Early American settlers boiled the roots and combed the resulting liquid through their hair to kill lice. The plant also goes by the locally common name Corn Lily.

167

Queen's Cup
Clintonia uniflora

LILY FAMILY

This beautiful perennial lily grows from slender rhizomes, with the flowers appearing on short, leafless stalks. The flowers are about 5 cm in diameter and are usually solitary, white, and cup-shaped, appearing at the top of an erect, hairy stem. The plant has two or three leaves, which are oblong or elliptical, shiny with hairy edges, and appear at the base of the flowering stem.

The genus name, *Clintonia*, honours DeWitt Clinton, a 19th-century New York state governor and botanist. As the season progresses, the flower is replaced by a single deep blue bead-like berry, giving the plant two other locally common names of Beadlily and Bluebead Lily. The bead was used by some Native peoples to make a blue dye.

Star-Flowered Solomon's-Seal
Maianthemum stellatum (formerly *Smilacina stellata*)

LILY FAMILY

This is a lily of moist woods, rivers and stream banks, thickets, and meadows, from montane to subalpine elevations. The flowers are white, star-shaped, and arrayed in a loose, short-stalked cluster, often on a zig-zag stem. The leaves are broadly lance-shaped, numerous, and alternate, gradually tapering to a pointed tip, with prominent parallel veining, sometimes folded at the midline. The fruit is a cluster of green- to cream-coloured berries, with maroon to brown stripes.

This plant was formerly in the genus *Smilacina*, but has now been moved to the genus *Maianthemum* as a result of molecular data establishing similarity to that different genus. *Maianthemum* is Latin for "May flower." One theory holds that the common name is a reference to the six-pointed star in the seal of King Solomon. The species name, *stellatum*, is Greek for "star-like." There is another closely related species found in the same habitat – False Solomon's-Seal (*M. racemosum*), shown on page 166. The flowers of False Solomon's-Seal are much more numerous, and decidedly smaller than those of Star-Flowered Solomon's-Seal. The flowers of False Solomon's-Seal were described by one observer as a "creamy foam of flowers," a rather apt description. Wild Lily-of-the-Valley (*M. canadense*) is another related species that occurs in the region. It has white flowers that appear in a cylindrical cluster, but its flowers have only four tepals, not six like other members of the genus.

Sticky False Asphodel (Northern Asphodel)
Tofieldia glutinosa

LILY FAMILY

A lily of wet bogs, meadows, and stream banks, this plant has a distinctive feature in the upper portion of its flowering stem, which is glandular and sticky. The white flowers are clustered atop the stem, with dark anthers conspicuous against the white of the petals. The basal leaves are linear, lance-shaped, and grass-like, and are about half the length of the stem.

The plant resembles the European Asphodel, thus the common name. The genus name, *Tofieldia*, is to honour 18th-century British botanist Thomas Tofield. The species name, *glutinosa*, is a reference to the sticky stem below the flower. Mosquitoes are often trapped on the sticky stem of this plant, which acts as natural flypaper. The plant also goes by the locally common name Northern Asphodel.

Three Spot Mariposa Lily (Three-Spot Tulip)
Calochortus apiculatus

LILY FAMILY

This perennial lily is a plant of open coniferous woods, dry, sandy, or gravelly slopes, and moist fescue grassland from the montane to the subalpine zone. It grows from a bulb as a single-leafed plant, producing one to five flowers from each plant. The flower is white to yellowish-white, with three spreading petals, fringed at the margins. Each petal is hairy on the inner surfaces, with a purplish gland at the base. These purple glands give the flower one of its common names, Three-Spot Tulip. Three narrow white sepals appear between the petals.

Mariposa means "butterfly" in Spanish, it being thought that the markings on some Mariposa lilies resemble the markings on a butterfly's wings. The genus name, *Calochortus*, is derived from the Greek *kallos*, meaning "beauty," and *chortos*, meaning "fodder" or "grass crop." The species name, *apiculatus*, refers to the slender tipped anthers. The plant also goes by the locally common name Pointedtip Mariposa Lily. Some Native tribes used the bulbs of the plant as food, whether raw, cooked, or dried for later use. The Blackfoot looked upon them as famine food only. Lyall's Butterfly Tulip (*C. lyallii*) is a similar plant that appears in the southern Okanagan. It also has a white flower, but it is distinguished by a moon-shaped spot on the inside base of the petals, with a broad purple crescent above it.

Western Trillium (Western Wake Robin)
Trillium ovatum

LILY FAMILY

This gorgeous lily blooms early and prefers boggy, rich soils in the montane and lower subalpine forests. The distinctive leaves are large (up to 15 cm long), stalkless, broadly egg-shaped with a sharp tip, and occur in a whorl of three below the flower. The solitary white flower blooms atop a short stem above the leaves. The flower has three broad white petals up to 5 cm long, alternating with three narrow green sepals. The petals change colour with age, first turning pink, and then progressing to purple.

The common and genus names are derived from the Latin *trillium*, meaning "in threes," a reference to the leaves, petals, and sepals occurring in threes. The species name, *ovatum*, refers to the shape of the leaves. The plant is an early bloomer, which gives rise to its other common name, Wake Robin, it being said that the blooms and the robins arrive about the same time in the spring. Seeds from the plant are oil rich and attract ants. Ants carry the seeds to their nests, and thus distribute the seeds for the plant. Some Native peoples referred to the plant as "Birth Root," a reference to using the plant to reduce uterine bleeding during childbirth. The plant was first described for science by Frederick Pursh from a specimen collected in 1806 by Meriwether Lewis "on the rapids of the Columbia River." Trillium is the floral emblem of the Province of Ontario.

White Camas
Zigadenus elegans

LILY FAMILY

This plant of moist grasslands, grassy slopes, and open woods grows from an onion-like bulb that has no oniony smell. The greenish-white, foul-smelling flowers appear in open clusters along an erect stem. There are yellowish-green V-shaped glands (nectaries) near the base of the petals and sepals. The leaves are mainly basal and resemble grass, with prominent midveins.

The origin of the genus name, *Zigadenus*, is explained in the narrative on Death Camas (*Z. venenosus*), shown on page 164. The species name, *elegans*, means "elegant." Though elegant indeed, these plants are also extremely poisonous, containing very toxic alkaloids, particularly in the bulbs. These plants have been responsible for killing many people and animals. When the flowers are missing, White Camas and Death Camas are difficult to distinguish from Early Camas (*Camassia quamash*), shown on page 91, another lily, the bulb of which was commonly used as food by Native peoples and early settlers. Other common names for White Camas include Mountain Death Camas, Green Lily, Elegant Poison Camas, Elegant Death Camas, and Showy Death Camas.

Northern Bedstraw
Galium boreale

MADDER FAMILY

This plant is common on roadsides and in woodlands in the montane to subalpine zones in the region. The flowers are tiny, fragrant, and white, occurring in dense clusters at the top of the stems. The individual flowers are cruciform (cross-shaped), with each having four spreading petals that are joined at the base. There are no sepals. The smooth stems are square in cross-section, and bear whorls of four narrow, lance-shaped leaves, each with three veins.

The genus name, *Galium*, is derived from the Greek *gala*, which means "milk," a reference to the fact that country folk used to use the juice of another similar plant to curdle milk. The species name, *boreale*, means "northern," a reference to the circumpolar distribution of the plant. The common name is a reference to a practice of Native peoples using the dried, sweet-smelling plants to stuff mattresses. The roots of the plants were a source of red and yellow dyes.

Sweet-Scented Bedstraw
Galium triflorum

MADDER FAMILY

This plant occurs in moist mountain forests, along stream banks, and in dense, damp woods. It is a low, trailing perennial that has leaves in whorls of six, radiating from a common centre stem. The leaves are tipped with a sharp point and have strongly hooked bristles on the underside. The leaves give off a sweet aroma, variously compared to vanilla or cinnamon. The flowers are small, greenish-white, and occur in groups of three in the leaf axils, with four petals per flower. The fruits are paired nutlets that are covered with hooked bristles.

The common name, Bedstraw, is derived from the practice of some Native peoples of using the plant for stuffing their mattresses. The plant also has the locally common name Sweet Woodruff. Another member of the genus, Northern Bedstraw (*G. boreale*), shown on page 174, occurs in similar habitat, and was used in the same fashion.

Morning Glory
Calystegia sepium (also *Convolvulus sepium*)

MORNING GLORY FAMILY

Morning Glory is a twining, climbing or trailing vine that grows from slender, spreading rhizomes. The flowers are 3–6 cm across, white to pinkish in colour and trumpet- or funnel-shaped. The leaves are alternate and arrowhead-shaped, and the flowers appear solitary in the leaf axils. The flowers usually close when it is dark, overcast or raining.

The genus name, *Calystegia*, is derived from the Greek *kalyx*, meaning "cup," and *stegos*, meaning "cover," a reference to the bracts that cover the sepals on the flower. This plant is also commonly called Hedge Bindweed, Lady's Nightcap, and Bell-Bind. A closely related plant, Field Bindweed (*C. arvensis*), is a noxious weed that creeps over crops and covers everything within its reach. Unlike many climbing plants, the Bindweeds cannot support their stems and tendrils, so they wind their stems tightly around available supports. Under favourable conditions, a Bindweed stem will complete an encirclement of a support in less than two hours time.

Field Pennycress (Stinkweed)
Thlaspi arvense

MUSTARD FAMILY

This member of the Mustard Family was introduced from Eurasia, and appears at low to middle elevations in cultivated areas and waste places. It blooms continuously from early spring until frosts arrive. The leaves have irregularly toothed margins, and clasp the stalk. The four-petalled white flowers appear in rounded clusters (racemes) at the tops of the stem.

The genus name, *Thlaspi*, is derived from the Greek *thlao*, which means "to crush," a reference to the fruits of the plant. The species name, *arvense*, is Latin meaning "of cultivated fields." The fruits of Pennycress are flat, circular pods with wide wings around the edges, and a notch at the top. The common name is derived from the resemblance of the fruits to the size of pennies. The plant has a strong, somewhat offensive odour when crushed, thus giving rise to another common name: Stinkweed.

Reflexed Rock Cress
Arabis holboellii

MUSTARD FAMILY

This plant is widespread in prairie zones, especially on gravelly slopes and in dry open woods. The plant stands up to 70 cm tall. The basal leaves form a rosette, and the stem leaves are numerous, narrow, lance-shaped, and clasping on the stem. The flowers are white to pinkish, occurring on reflexed stalks, hanging down along the stem and in a terminal cluster.

The genus name, *Arabis*, is said to have originated in Arabia, where numerous Rock Cresses occur. The species name, *holboellii*, is to honour 19th-century Danish botanist Carl Peter Holbøll. Rock Cresses are edible and are said to have a taste similar to radishes. The leaves and flowers are often added to salads and sandwiches. The common name cress is said to be derived from an old Indo-European word that meant "to eat" or "nibble." A similar species, Drummond's Rock Cress (*A. drummondii*), occurs in similar habitat, but is shorter, and holds its pods erect or slightly spreading. Lyall's Rock Cress (*A. lyallii*) also occurs in the area, but it is a subalpine or alpine species and has small pale purple flowers.

Stinging Nettle
Urtica dioica

NETTLE FAMILY

This plant occurs in moist mountain forests, thickets, and meadows at various elevations. The plant has a square stem and can grow to 2 m tall. The leaves are narrowly lance-shaped, opposite, simple, toothed, and appear wrinkled. The leaves are shiny on top, up to 15 cm long, tapered to the tip, and covered with small hairs. The flowers are inconspicuous, green, and occur in drooping clusters from the leaf axils. Both male and female flowers appear on the same plant.

The genus name, *Urtica*, is derived from the Latin *uro*, meaning "to burn," a very understandable reference to anybody who has had the misfortune of getting involved with the stinging hairs that cover this plant. Interestingly, despite the nasty skin irritation that can result from casual contact, the leaves of the plant are considered important both as a food and as a medicine. The plant is rendered harmless when cooked. Modern herbalists value the plant as an astringent and a diuretic. Native peoples often used the stems of mature plants for making string and other cordage material.

Alaska Rein-Orchid
Piperia unalascensis

ORCHID FAMILY

Virginia Skilton image

This orchid grows up to 90 cm tall from an egg-shaped tuber at low to middle elevations in dry to moist forests and open, rocky, dry slopes. The plant has two to five lance-shaped basal leaves that are up to 15 cm long and 4 cm wide, which usually wither prior to the flowers blooming. The inflorescence is a spike-like spirally arranged raceme at the top of the stem. The small flowers are greenish to white, moderately fragrant, and have a triangular lip with a spur of about equal size.

The genus name, *Piperia*, honours Charles Vancouver Piper, an early 20th-century Canadian-born agronomist and botanist who worked for the United States Department of Agriculture. The species name, *unalascensis*, refers to the Aleutian island Unalaska, where the plant was first found. The plant also goes by the locally common name of Slender-Spire Orchid. Elegant Rein-Orchid (*P. elegans*) is a similar species that occurs in similar habitat. It has a spur that is about twice as long as the lip.

Heart-Leaved Twayblade
Listera cordata

ORCHID FAMILY

This small orchid, standing about 20 cm tall, prefers a cool, damp, mossy habitat. As a consequence of its size and preferred location, it is an easy flower to miss. The white flowers are scattered up the stem in an open raceme. The lip of the flower in this species is deeply split, almost in two. The stem leaf structure of the genus is distinctive, with two leaves appearing opposite to each other part way up the stem.

The common name, Twayblade, refers to the two stem leaves. The genus name, *Listera*, commemorates Dr. Martin Lister, an English naturalist of the 1600s. The species name, *cordata*, means "heart-shaped," a reference to the shape of the stem leaves. Several other Twayblades appear in the same habitat. All are relatively rare, and they all have two leaves held flat and opposite about halfway up the stem. Northwest Twayblade (*L. caurina*) has larger leaves than this species, and a larger lip that is not notched at the tip.

Hooded Ladies' Tresses
Spiranthes romanzoffiana

ORCHID FAMILY

This orchid is reasonably common in swampy places, meadows, open shady woods and lakeshores and can stand up to 60 cm tall. The characteristic feature of the plant is the crowded flower spike, which can contain up to 60 densely spaced white flowers that appear to coil around the end of the stem in three spiraling ranks. When newly bloomed, the flower has a wonderful aroma, which most people say smells like vanilla.

The common name of the plant is a reference to the braid-like appearance of the flowers, similar to a braid in a lady's hair. The genus name is derived from the Greek *speira*, meaning "coil," and *anthos*, meaning "flower," referring to the spiral inflorescence. The species name honours Count Nikolai Romanzoff, a 19th-century Russian minister of state and patron of science. The species was first discovered on the Aleutian island of Unalaska, when Alaska was still a Russian territory.

Mountain Lady's Slipper
Cypripedium montanum

ORCHID FAMILY

This distinctive orchid grows up to 60 cm tall, and occurs in dry to moist woods and open areas from middle to subalpine elevations. The lower petal forms a white, pouch-shaped lower lip that has purple markings. The sepals and lateral petals are brownish, have wavy margins, and appear to spiral away from the stem. The attractive leaves are alternate, broadly elliptical, clasping on the stem, and have prominent veins. One to three flowers appear on the stem, and they are wonderfully fragrant.

The genus name, *Cypripedium*, is derived from the Greek *kupris*, meaning "Aphrodite," the Greek goddess of love and beauty, and *pedilon*, meaning "foot" or "slipper," thus Aphrodite's slipper. The species name, *montanum*, means "of the mountains." This plant is relatively rare in its natural habitat, but has been made more so by indiscriminate picking and attempts at transplantation, which virtually never are successful. The plant depends upon the flower for nutrition, and picking the flower will kill the plant. Two other Lady's Slippers occur in the region. Yellow Lady's Slipper (*C. parviflorum*), is shown on page 47. Sparrow's-Egg Lady's Slipper (*C. passerinum*), shown on page 186, also known as Franklin's Lady's Slipper, occurs in the southeastern portions of the region. It is smaller than either of the other two Lady's Slippers, and is white with purple spots, said to resemble a sparrow's egg.

One-Leaved Rein-Orchid
Platanthera obtusata (formerly *Habenaria obtusata*)

ORCHID FAMILY

The solitary leaf and small, greenish-white flowers of this orchid make it easy to distinguish from other local orchids. The single, basal leaf is oblong and blunt on the end, tapering to the sheathing base. The stem grows up to about 20 cm tall, with the flowers distributed up the stem. The flowers have a strap-shaped lip, and a tapering spur which is about as long as the lip.

The genus name, *Platanthera*, is Latin for "flat anthers." The former genus name, *Habenaria*, is derived from the Latin *habena*, meaning "rein," a reference to the rein-like appendages on the lip, hence the source of the common name. The species name, *obtusata,* means "blunt," a reference to the shape of the single leaf. Indeed, another locally common name for the plant is Blunt-Leaved Orchid. The species is pollinated by mosquitoes, which are usually in no short supply in the habitat of this lovely orchid, mossy forests, bogs, and swamps. Round-Leaved Rein-Orchid (*P. orbiculata*) is a similar species that grows in similar habitat. It has two round, glossy, clasping, opposite leaves at the base of the flowering stem.

Round-Leaved Orchid
Amerorchis rotundifolia (formerly *Orchis rotundifolia*)

ORCHID FAMILY

This tiny orchid, standing no more than 25 cm tall, occurs in well-drained parts of bogs and swamps and in cold, moist, mossy coniferous forests. The flowers are irregular, with three white to pink sepals. The upper sepal combines with the upper two, purple-veined petals to form a hood. The two lateral sepals are wing-like. The lowest petal forms a white to pink oblong lip, spotted with dark red or purple markings. The leaf is basal, solitary, and broadly elliptic.

The genus name is derived from the Greek *orchis*, meaning "testicle," because the swollen tubers of the species resemble testicles. As a result of this, orchids were once thought to be a powerful aphrodisiac for both people and animals. The species name, *rotundifolia*, means "round leafed." These small orchids are always a treat to discover, and in some places they appear in profusion. This plant should not be confused with Round-Leaved Rein-Orchid (*Platanthera orbiculata*), which is another orchid that grows in the region, but it is quite a different plant. It more resembles One-Leaved Rein-Orchid (*P. obtusata*), shown on page 184.

Sparrow's-Egg Lady's Slipper (Franklin's Lady's Slipper)
Cypripedium passerinum

ORCHID FAMILY

This lovely orchid grows from a cord-like rhizome in boggy areas, along streams, and in mossy coniferous areas. It resembles both Yellow Lady's Slipper (*C. parviflorum*), shown on page 47, and Mountain Lady's Slipper (*C. montanum*), shown on page 183, in shape, but this flower is smaller, has bright purple dots on the interior, and has shorter, stubbier, greenish sepals. Both the stem and the leaves of the plant are covered in soft hairs.

The origin of the genus name is explained in the note on Mountain Lady's Slipper. The species name, *passerinum*, means "sparrow-like," a reference to the spotting on the flower being like the markings on a sparrow egg. Care should be taken when moving around these orchids. They are fragile and easily damaged. Picking the flower is anathema – the flower will quickly wilt, and the plant will die without the nutrition provided by the flower.

Western Rattlesnake Plantain
Goodyera oblongifolia

ORCHID FAMILY

This orchid grows in shaded, dry or moist coniferous woods in the mountains. It is a single-stemmed, stiff-hairy perennial that grows up to 40 cm tall. The basal leaves are distinctive, with a white, mottled midvein, and whitish lateral veins. The robust downy spike bears small greenish-white flowers in a loose, one-sided or twisted raceme, with the lower flowers blooming first. The lip of the flower has a wide-open mouth pressed up against the overhanging hood.

The common name originates from the mottled white markings on the leaves, which reminded early European settlers of the markings on a rattlesnake. Plantain comes from the Latin *planta*, meaning "foot," a reference to the broad, flat, foot-like leaves. The genus name commemorates the 17th-century English botanist John Goodyer.

White Bog Orchid (Tall White Bog Orchid)
Platanthera dilatata (formerly *Habenaria dilatata*)

ORCHID FAMILY

As the common name suggests, this plant favours wet ground, shaded woods, bogs, pond edges, and streamside environments. It grows up to 1 m tall, and produces white to greenish, sweet-scented flowers in a spike-like cluster, with flowers distributed along the stalk. The flowers are waxy and small, with the lowest petal forming a lip that widens at the base. The flower also has a slender, curved spur. The lance-shaped leaves are prominently veined and fleshy, short at the base, longest in the middle of the plant, and shorter at the top.

The origin of the genus name, *Platanthera*, is discussed in the note on One-Leaved Rein-Orchid (*P. obtusata*), shown on page 184. The species name, *dilatata*, means "dilated," a reference to the expanded base of the lip on the flower. When blooming, this flower has a heavenly scent, variously described as of vanilla, mock orange, or cloves. Indeed, two locally common names for the plant are Fragrant White Rein Orchid and Fragrant White Bog Orchid. Some Native peoples believed the plant to be poisonous to humans and animals, and used an extract from it to sprinkle on baits for coyotes and grizzlies. Green-Flowered Bog Orchid (*P. hyperborea*) is a similar species that occurs in similar habitat. It has green flowers and fewer leaves than this species.

Creamy Peavine (Cream Pea)
Lathyrus ochroleucus

PEA FAMILY

Virginia Skilton image

A plant of moist shaded woods, thicket edges, and stream banks, this twining perennial grows up to 1 m long and has coiled tendrils at the ends of the leaves with which it climbs on adjacent plants. The leaves are alternate and compound, with 6–10 leaflets per leaf. The leaflets are oval, pointed at the tip, smooth, and often display a whitish bloom. The flowers are pale yellow to white, and pea-like, occurring in loose clusters from the leaf axils.

Lathyrus is the ancient Greek name for a kind of Spurge. The species name, *ochroleucus*, is also Greek, meaning "yellowish white," alluding to the flower colour. There is also a purple-flowered Peavine (*L. venosus*). in the same habitat and range. The Peavines are distinguished from the Vetches by their larger leaves and stipules, and by having a style that is hairy along one side of its length, like a toothbrush. The style in Vetches is hairy around its tip, like a bottle brush.

White Sweet-Clover
Melilotus alba

PEA FAMILY

A plant of roadsides, ditches, embankments, and pastures, this introduced plant is quite common. It grows to over 2 m tall, with smooth, leafy, branched stems. The leaflets are slightly toothed, and appear in threes. The flowers are white, and appear in long, narrow, tapered clusters at the top of the plant and in the leaf axils. Each individual flower has a typical pea shape, with standard, wings, and a keel. In this flower the standard and wings are about the same length, and the wings are attached to the keel.

The genus name, *Melilotus*, is derived from the Greek *meli*, meaning "honey," and *lotos*, the name of some clover-like plant in the Mediterranean. *Alba* is Latin meaning "white." This plant, and a similar one called Yellow Sweet-Clover (*M. officinalis*), were introduced as forage for livestock. Both plants contain coumarin, which imparts an overwhelmingly sweet fragrance when you are near the plants or when they are cut for hay.

Wild Licorice
Glycyrrhiza lepidota

PEA FAMILY

This coarse perennial grows up to 1 m tall from a thick rootstock that has a slight licorice flavour, and occurs in moist grasslands, along stream and riverbanks, and in slough margins and disturbed areas. The leaves are alternate and pinnately compound, with 11 to 19 pale green, sharply pointed, lance-shaped leaflets. The leaflets have glandular dots on the underside, and produce a lemony odour when crushed. The flowers are yellowish-white, numerous, showy, and occur in dense clusters at the top of the stem. The flowers are typically of members of the Pea Family, and have an upward pointing standard that encloses the wings and keel. The flower cluster blooms from the bottom up. The fruits are densely clustered, oblong, flattened reddish pods, that are covered with hooked barbs.

The genus name, *Glycyrrhiza*, is derived from the Greek *glykyrrhiza*, which means "sweet root." The species name, *lepidota*, means "scaly," and refers to the glands on the underside of the leaves. Native peoples roasted and ate the roots of the plant, and also used it medicinally to treat a variety of ailments.

Hood's Phlox
Phlox hoodii

PHLOX FAMILY

This is a plant of dry, exposed hillsides, eroded slopes, foothills and prairies. The small five-petalled flowers with orange stamens are united into a tube below. The leaves are awl-shaped with spiny tips, tiny and overlapping, grey-green and woolly at the base. The plant grows low to the ground and covers the ground like a moss. The flowers show a tremendous variance in colour, from white to all shades of blue and purple.

The genus name, *Phlox*, is Greek for "flame," a reference to the vivid colours of some members of the genus. The species name, *hoodii*, honours Robert Hood, a midshipman on one of Sir John Franklin's expeditions to find the Northwest Passage. This flower blooms early in the spring and adds a wonderful spectrum of colour to an otherwise drab landscape. Spreading Phlox (*P. diffusa*) is a very similar plant that grows in the region. It is also a mat-forming plant which has showy white flowers, though the colour may vary. The specific identification of members of the *Phlox* genus can be difficult and may require measurements, magnification, and dissection.

Mouse-Ear Chickweed (Field Chickweed)
Cerastium arvense

PINK FAMILY

This early-blooming plant thrives in dry grasslands and rocky and disturbed ground, often forming large mats of white flowers in the spring. The white flowers appear in loose clusters, often many flowers to each plant. The five white petals are notched and have green lines on them as nectar guides for insects.

The upper part of the leaf resembles a mouse's ear, thus the common name for the plant. The genus name, *Cerastium*, is derived from the Greek *keras*, meaning "horn," a reference to the shape of the seed capsule. The species name, *arvense*, means "of cultivated fields."

Night-Flowering Catchfly
Silene noctiflora

PINK FAMILY

This plant was introduced from Europe and has become a common and troublesome noxious weed in some areas. It is an erect, branching plant that grows up to 90 cm tall in ditches, waste areas, and field edges. The leaves, stems, and flowers are sticky and hairy. The leaves are opposite, dark green, and lance-shaped. The flowers are white and fragrant, with the sepals united to form a sticky, oval, tubular, swollen calyx that is up to 2 cm long and handsomely striped with white and green. The five petals are deeply cleft at the ends. The flowers open in the evening to attract moths and other night-flying insects, then close in the morning.

The genus name, *Silene*, is derived from the Greek *sialon*, which means "saliva," a reference to the sticky, glandular hairs on the plant. Those sticky hairs probably also give rise to the common name Catchfly. The species name, *noctiflora*, reflects the habit of the flowers to open only at night. This plant can be confused with White Cockle (*Lychnis alba*), which also occurs in the same habitat and has similarly constructed flowers. White Cockle is not sticky when squeezed.

Starflower
Trientalis latifolia

PRIMROSE FAMILY

This plant appears at low to middle elevations in shady, moist forests, forest openings, and seepage sites. The small pink to white saucer-shaped corolla is deeply divided into six or seven sharply pointed lobes. Each flower is borne on a thin, curved stalk that rises from the centre of the leaf whorl. The leaves are oval elliptic and grow in a whorl at the top of a stem that grows low to the ground. The fruits are round white cases that resemble tiny soccer balls.

The genus name, *Trientalis*, is Latin for "one third of a foot," which aptly describes the height of the plant. The species name also is Latin, meaning "broad-leaved." The common name, Starflower, has been applied because the flowers grow on a very slender stalk, leaving them apparently hanging in the air like tiny stars.

Western Spring Beauty
Claytonia lanceolata

PURSLANE FAMILY

This plant grows from a marble-sized corm and is widely scattered in the region at middle to high elevations on moist, grassy slopes and meadows. The flowers of this early-blooming plant are white, but may appear pink, owing to the reddish veins in the petals and the pink anthers. The tips of the petals are distinctly notched. The plants are usually less than 20 cm tall, and the flowers appear in loose, terminal short-stalked clusters.

The genus name, Claytonia, honours John Clayton, a 17th-century botanist who collected plants in what was to become the United States. The species name, *lanceolata*, refers to the lance-shaped leaves. The corm of the plant was used by Native peoples as food. In fact, another locally common name for the plant is Indian Potato, it being said that the corms of the plant taste like potatoes. Bears and rodents also make use of the corms of the plant for food. Ungulates often eat the flowers and leaves. Alpine Spring Beauty (*C. megarhiza*) is a relatively rare but similar plant that occurs in the alpine zone. It has spoon-shaped, reddish-green, basal leaves and grows not from a corm but from a taproot.

Birch-Leaf Spirea
Spiraea betulifolia

ROSE FAMILY

This deciduous shrub grows up to 70 cm tall in moist to dry, open and wooded sites from valley floors to the subalpine zone. It spreads by underground runners, and often forms dense cover on the forest floor. The plant is alternately branched, with cinnamon-brown bark, and alternate oval or egg-shaped leaves that are irregularly coarse-toothed toward the tip. The flowers are dull white, often tinged to purple or pink, saucer-shaped, and occur in flat-topped clusters on the ends of the stems.

The genus name, *Spiraea*, is from the Greek *speira*, which means "twisted," or "wound together," possibly a reference to plants of this genus being used as garlands. The species name, *betulifolia*, means "leaves like a birch," the reference being to the similarity of Spirea leaves to those of birch trees. Two common names for the plant are White Spirea and White Meadowsweet. Native peoples and herbalists have long used the plant to relieve pain, reduce inflammations, and treat a variety of other ailments, from heartburn to abdominal and menstrual pains. The branches of the plant were also used for drying and smoking fish. A similar species, Mountain or Subalpine Spirea (*S. densiflora*), also known as Pink Meadowsweet, occurs infrequently in middle to subalpine elevations in the region. It has rose- to pink-coloured, flat-topped clusters of flowers.

197

Black Hawthorn
Crataegus douglasii

ROSE FAMILY

This is a large deciduous shrub that can reach up to 8 m in height. The bark is grey, rough, and scaly, and the plant has sharp, stout thorns up to 3 cm long that will command immediate attention from the unwary passerby who stumbles into the plant. The leaves are oval-shaped and appear leathery, with multiple lobes at the top. The flowers are white, showy, and saucer-shaped, occurring in clusters at the tips of the branches. The berries are generally unpalatable dark purplish pomes that contain a large, hard seed.

The genus name, *Crataegus*, is derived from the Greek *kratos*, meaning "strength," a reference to the hard, fine-grained wood of the plant. The common name is derived from the Anglo-Saxon word *haguthorn*, which was "a fence with thorns," referring to the use of this plant as a hedge. Native peoples used the thorns from the plant for various purposes, including probing blisters and boils, fish hooks, and piercing ears. The wood of the plant was used for making tool and weapon handles. The bark from the plant was used medicinally by some Native peoples for treatment of diarrhea and stomach pains. Modern herbalists value Hawthorn berries as a tonic for the treatment of high blood pressure.

Chokecherry
Prunus virginiana

ROSE FAMILY

This plant is a conspicuous white-flowering shrub or small tree that is common in thickets, open woods, and along streams. The five-petalled saucer-shaped flowers are borne in thick cylindrical clusters. The fruit is a red-purple to black berry that is almost all pit. The fruit appears in dense clusters at the terminal ends of branches.

Prunus is Latin for "plum tree." Most people find the fruit of the Chokecherry too bitter to eat raw, thus the common name. The fruits can be processed to produce quite acceptable jelly, syrup, and wine. Birds and mammals seem to relish the fruits. Bears are often drawn to large congregations of Chokecherries and will work over the bushes until the fruits are gone. Ungulates such as elk and deer forage on the leaves and twigs of the plant. New growth, wilted leaves, and plant parts injured by frosts or drought are poisonous to livestock and humans. The toxin is hydrocyanic acid, a form of cyanide which can make breathing difficult, lowers pulse, and causes staggering and loss of consciousness. The toxicity is highest in spring and early summer, but the plant is generally safe by the time the fruits mature. At least one authority cautions against inhaling the smoke from burned Chokecherry wood. Native peoples used the wood for fashioning tool handles, and, interestingly enough, some made a decoction from the bark which they drank as a tonic.

Ocean Spray (Cream Bush)
Holodiscus discolor

ROSE FAMILY

This is an erect, loosely branched deciduous shrub that grows to over 3 m tall on bluffs and in dry to moist woods. The leaves are ovate, up to 8 cm long, lobed, toothed, and woolly-hairy underneath. The flowers are large pyramidal clusters of tiny white flowers that occur at the branch ends. The plant is aptly named. The clusters of white flowers bring to mind the foam cast about by crashing waves and ocean winds. The plant has a sweet scent from a distance, but is said to be musty smelling in close proximity.

The genus name, *Holodiscus*, is derived from the Greek *holo*, which means "whole," and *discus*, which means "disk," a reference to the placement of the flower parts. The species name, *discolor*, is derived from the Latin *dis*, which in this context means "two," most probably a reference to the fact that the white flowers turn brown as they wither. The wood of the plant is exceptionally hard and strong. Native peoples used it to fashion a number of tools, including arrows, harpoons, digging implements, anchor pins for tepees, awls, etc. The wood does not burn readily, so it was also used for the manufacture of cooking tools and spits for roasting salmon.

Partridgefoot (Creeping Spiraea)
Luetkea pectinata

ROSE FAMILY

This dwarf evergreen shrub creates extensive mats as it creeps over the ground in moist meadows, scree slopes, and shady areas near timberline. It often grows where snow melts late in the season. The leaves are mainly basal, numerous, smooth, fan-shaped, and much divided. Old leaves wither and persist for long periods of time. The white to cream-coloured flowers appear in short, crowded clusters atop erect stems. The flowers have four to six pistils, and about 20 stamens, which are conspicuous on the flowers.

The genus name, *Luetkea*, honours Count F.P. Lütke, a 19th-century Russian sea captain and explorer. This is the only species in the genus. The species name, *pectinata*, means "with narrow divisions – like the teeth of a comb," and is a reference to the structure of the leaves. The common name, Partridgefoot, is derived from the supposed resemblance between the leaves of the species and the footprint of a partridge. Given the subalpine and alpine habitat of this plant, it might be more appropriately called Ptarmiganfoot.

Red Raspberry
Rubus idaeus

ROSE FAMILY

This erect to spreading deciduous shrub grows up to 2 m tall at low to subalpine elevations in clearings, along streams, and in disturbed areas. It is similar to cultivated raspberry in appearance. The prickly branches, or canes, are biennial, and are green in the first year and yellowish brown to cinnamon brown in the second. The leaves are palmately divided (i.e., divided into leaflets that diverge from a common point) into three to five egg-shaped, pointed, double saw-toothed leaflets. The flowers are white and drooping, occurring singly or in small clusters. The fruits are juicy red drupelets – a drupelet being one part of an aggregate fruit – in dense clusters, the totality of which is the raspberry. Other examples of fruits that appear as drupelets include blackberries and thimbleberries.

Native peoples made extensive use of the plant as food and for medicinal purposes. A tea brewed from the plant was administered to women to ease the pain of childbirth, and the concoction was also used to treat a variety of other conditions such as boils, bladder infections, liver problems, and diarrhea. Modern herbalists also value this plant for a variety of conditions. Pharmacologists have validated raspberry leaf as an antispasmodic.

202

Saskatoon (Serviceberry)
Amelanchier alnifolia

ROSE FAMILY

This deciduous shrub grows up to 5 m tall or more, and is found in open woods, on stream banks, and hillsides, from the prairie to montane elevations. The shrub is erect to spreading, with smooth bark that is reddish when new, turning greyish with age. The leaves are alternate, oval to round in shape, rounded at the tips, and coarsely toothed on the upper half. The white flowers are star-shaped, with five slender petals, about 2 cm across, and occur in clusters near the branch tips. The petals are wider above the middle, and taper to a slender base. The fruits are sweet and juicy berry-like pomes – like tiny apples – purple to black when ripe.

The genus name, *Amelanchier*, is an Old French common name for a similar Old World species. The species name, *alnifolia*, is Latin meaning "leaves like alders." Saskatoons were one of the most important berries for Native peoples. They were eaten fresh or were dried for later use. They were also mashed and dried into large cakes. The Lewis and Clark Expedition reported some of these cakes weighed as much as 7 kg. The dried fruits were often added to meats, soups, and stews. The hard, straight branches of the plant were also used for manufacturing arrow shafts, basket rims, canoe parts, and tepee stakes and closures. The plants are also important browse for elk, moose, and deer, and the berries are eaten by bears, small mammals, and birds. During the Great Depression, the Saskatoon was the only fruit known to thousands of prairie dwellers. Other common names for the plant include Juneberry, Serviceberry, and Shadbush.

Thimbleberry
Rubus parviflorus

ROSE FAMILY

This is a plant that often forms thickets on avalanche slopes and at the margins of forests and streams. The plant is closely related to the raspberry, but this vigorous shrub does not have prickles or spines. The plant can grow up to 2 m tall. It has large leaves, each with three to five lobes, with jagged-toothed margins, resembling a maple leaf in shape. The flowers are white, with a central core of yellow stamens. There are usually three to five flowers in clusters at the ends of branches. The bright red fruit looks like a flattened raspberry but it is rather tasteless and very seedy.

The origin of the genus name, *Rubus*, is explained in the note on Dwarf Raspberry (*R. arcticus*), shown on page 281. The specific name, *parviflorus*, is derived from Greek *parvus*, which means "small," and the Latin *flora*, which means "flower," ergo, small-flowered. The name is puzzling given that Thimbleberry flowers are not at all small in the scheme of things. Native peoples peeled the young shoots of Thimbleberry and ate them raw, or cooked them with meat in stews. The large leaves were widely used as temporary containers, to line baskets, and to separate items in the same basket. They also make a good biodegradable toilet tissue substitute when needed.

Trailing Raspberry
Rubus pubescens

ROSE FAMILY

This dwarf shrub is a low, trailing plant with slender runners and erect flowering stems that grows at low to subalpine elevations in moist to wet forests and clearings. The plant has soft hairs on it, but no prickles like wild Red Raspberry (*R. idaeus*), shown on page 202. The leaves are palmately divided into three oval or diamond-shaped leaflets, with pointed tips and toothed margins. The flowers are white and spreading, and occur on short, erect branches. The fruits are red drupelets – the aggregate cluster makes up a raspberry.

Native peoples used this plant as food and for medicinal purposes, similarly to Red Raspberry. Trailing Raspberry is also known by the locally common names Dewberry, Dwarf Red Blackberry, and Dwarf Red Raspberry.

Western Mountain Ash
Sorbus scopulina

ROSE FAMILY

This deciduous, erect to spreading shrub grows to 4 m tall in moist open or shaded places from the foothills to the subalpine zones. The branches are slightly white-hairy and sticky when new; reddish-grey to yellowish when mature. The leaves are alternate and pinnately compound – leaflets appearing opposite each other on both sides of a common axis – with 11 to 13 leaflets per leaf. The leaflets are sharply tipped and sharply toothed from tip to base. The flowers are white and saucer-shaped, with five broad petals, and they occur in large flat-topped clusters. The fruits are glossy orange to red berry-like pomes in dense clusters.

The origin of the genus name, *Sorbus*, is a matter of some contention. It was either the Latin name for mountain ash, or was the Greek name for oak, depending on which authority you choose to follow. The species name, *scopulina*, means "growing in rocky places." Some Native peoples ate the pomes of this plant, but most looked upon them as inedible. Some tribes boiled the peeled branches or inner bark of the plant to make medicinal concoctions. The plant is used quite extensively as a garden ornamental. The fruit clusters are a favoured food of a variety of bird species.

White Dryad (White Mountain Avens)
Dryas octopetala

ROSE FAMILY

Doug Skilton image

This dwarf evergreen grows close to the ground, forming mats on gravelly soil in the alpine zone. The leaves are oblong to lance-shaped, leathery, dark green, with edges that are scalloped and often rolled under. The creamy-coloured flowers bloom in abundance soon after snows melt. The flowers are borne on short, hairy, leafless stems that rise from the mats of leaves. Each flower has eight petals, thus the species name *octopetala*. The fruits are similar to those of the Drummond's Mountain Avens (*D. drummondii*), shown on page 54.

The genus is named after Dryas, the wood nymph in Greek mythology. This plant is superbly adapted to its harsh natural environment. The plant has root nodules that store nitrogen in a nutrient-poor habitat. White Dryad is also valued by rock-gardeners as a ground cover.

Wild Strawberry
Fragaria virginiana

ROSE FAMILY

This is a plant of shaded to open gravelly soils and thickets from prairie to alpine habitats. The single five-petalled white flower appears on a leafless stem that is usually shorter than the leaves are long. The stamens are numerous and yellow. The leaves are rounded to broadly oval, toothed, with three leaflets on short stalks. The fruit is a red berry covered with sunken, seed-like achenes. New plants are often established from reddish runners.

Strawberry is said to come from the Anglo-Saxon name *streowberie* because the runners from the plant are strewn across the ground. The genus name, *Fragaria*, means "fragrance." Strawberry plants are rich in iron, calcium, potassium, sodium, and vitamin C. The fruits are delicious, with a more pronounced flavour than domestic strawberries. The leaves have been used to make tea, and have also been used for medicinal purposes.

Pale Comandra (Bastard Toadflax)
Comandra umbellata

SANDALWOOD FAMILY

This erect, blue-green perennial is common in open pine woods, gravel slopes, and grasslands. It springs from a creeping rootstock and has lance-shaped leaves which hug the erect stem. The flowers occur in a rounded or flat-topped cluster atop the stem. Each flower is greenish-white, with the sepals separated above, and fused into a small funnel below.

The genus name, *Comandra*, is derived from the Greek *kome*, meaning "hair," and *andros*, meaning "man," probably a reference to the hairy bases of the stamens on the flower. The species name, *umbellata*, is Latin, a reference to the shape of the cluster of flowers. The plant has another common name – Bastard Toadflax – though the plant bears no relationship to Toadflax and is not in any way similar. Pale Comandra is a parasite, taking water and perhaps food from its host plant.

Alaska Saxifrage (Rusty Saxifrage)
Saxifraga ferruginea

SAXIFRAGE FAMILY

This plant grows in moist soils, on rocky outcrops, and along spring banks in the subalpine and alpine zones. The leaves are basal only, hairy, and wedge-shaped with toothed margins. The numerous white flowers bloom in an open inflorescence on hairy stems. The flowers have five petals. The three upper petals are broader than the lower two petals, have yellow spots, and abruptly narrow at the base. Some of the flowers on the plant may become leafy bulblets and drop off the plant.

The genus name, *Saxifraga*, is derived from the Latin *saxum*, meaning "rock," and *frangere*, meaning "to break," a reference to the belief that plants in the genus are capable of breaking rocks into soil. The species name, *ferruginea*, is derived from the Latin *ferrum*, which means "iron," a reference to the rusty colour of the calyx. That rusty colour gives rise to another common name, Rusty Saxifrage.

Bishop's Cap (Bare-Stemmed Mitrewort)
Mitella nuda

SAXIFRAGE FAMILY

This wonderful plant occurs in moist to dry forests, bogs, thickets, and along streams, from the aspen parklands to the subalpine elevations. The plant stands erect and grows up to 20 cm tall. The leaves are basal, heart to kidney-shaped, and short-lobed, with rounded teeth. The flowers are tiny, and occur in an open cluster, scattered up the leafless stem. The saucer-shaped flowers are very distinctive, and when examined closely remind one of some kind of a satellite dish, complete with antennae festooned around the circumference of the flower.

The genus name, *Mitella*, is derived from the Greek *mitra*, which means "a cap," a reference to the flower's resemblance to a mitre – the hat worn by bishops – hence the common name Bishop's Cap. The species name, *nuda*, means "naked," most probably a reference to the leafless stem of the plant. This plant is one of the most fascinating in the forest. A number of Mitreworts appear in the region. They all are similar in terms of basic flower configuration. Mitreworts are often referred to as Snowflakes because the flowers are reminiscent of the intricate designs of snowflakes.

Foamflower (False Mitrewort)
Tiarella trifoliata var. *unifoliata*

SAXIFRAGE FAMILY

These beautiful flowers inhabit moist coniferous woods, stream banks and trails from low to subalpine elevations. The plant grows up to 50 cm tall, and the flowers are white or pinkish, arranged in open panicles well above the leaves. The stamens protrude from the petals, giving the plant a foamy appearance. The leaves are compound, usually with three leaflets. The middle leaflet is usually three-lobed and toothed.

The genus name, *Tiarella*, is derived from the Latin *tiara*, an ancient Persian, turban-like headdress. The species name, *trifoliata*, refers to the compound leaf with three leaflets. Other common names applied to the plant are Laceflower and False Mitrewort.

Fringe Cup
Tellima grandiflora

SAXIFRAGE FAMILY

This plant grows from scaly rhizomes in moist woods, along streams, and in avalanche chutes at low to middle elevations. The long-stalked basal leaves are heart-shaped, 8 cm wide and about as long, irregularly toothed, scalloped on the margin and covered with white hairs. The flowering stems stand 80 cm tall and the flowers occur in a one-sided spike-like terminal cluster of 10 to 35 nodding blooms. The individual flowers have five greenish-white petals that are fringed at the tips. The flowers usually turn pinkish or reddish with age.

The genus name, *Tellima*, is an anagram for *Mitella*, a genus within the Saxifrage Family, the plants of which are generally referred to as Mitreworts. (Bishop's Cap (*M. nuda*) is shown on page 211.) The species name, *grandiflora*, means "large flowered," which is puzzling given that the flowers of Fringe Cup are only 1–1.5 cm long.

Leather-Leaved Saxifrage
Leptarrhena pyrolifolia

SAXIFRAGE FAMILY

This plant occurs in wet, open forests, wet meadows, along streams, and in seeps in the subalpine and alpine zones. The leaves are mostly basal, oval to oblong, leathery, prominently veined, and have toothed edges. The purplish stems are erect, up to 40 cm tall, and have only one to three small leaves. The flowers are small and white, sometimes pink, and appear in tight clusters at the top of the flowering stem. Each flower has ten long stamens. The fruits of the plant are perhaps more striking than the flowers. The fruits are paired, pointed, purplish-red, single-chambered capsules in clusters atop the stem.

The genus name, *Leptarrhena*, is derived from the Greek *leptos*, which means "slender," and *arren*, which means "male," a reference to the slender stamens on the plant. The species name, *pyrolifolia*, most probably is a reference to the leaves, *Pyrola* being the genus of many Wintergreens, which have leathery leaves. This plant has been enthusiastically adopted by rock gardeners.

Red-Stemmed Saxifrage
Saxifraga lyallii

SAXIFRAGE FAMILY

This plant occurs on stream banks, seepage areas, and other wet places in the high subalpine and alpine zones, and is often found growing in wet mosses at such elevations. The leaves are basal, fan- to wedge-shaped, coarsely toothed, and abruptly narrowing on long stalks. The flowering stems grow up to 30 cm tall, and each bears one to several tiny, white, star-shaped flowers on its upper parts. When mature, the white petals are marked with greenish-yellow blotches, and the sepals are reflexed. The fruits are two- to four-pointed, bright red capsules.

The origin of the genus name, *Saxifraga*, is discussed in the note on Alaska Saxifrage (*S. ferruginea*), shown on page 210. The plant is also known as Lyall's Saxifrage, named in honour of David Lyall, a 19th-century Scottish botanist who collected a number of North American plants. As a group, Saxifrages have some of the most intricate and interesting flower conformations in the region, and all are worth examining closely.

Round-Leaved Alumroot
Heuchera cylindrica

SAXIFRAGE FAMILY

This robust perennial can grow up to 1 m tall, and can be widespread and common on dry plateaus, open forests, and rocky outcrops. The leaves are all basal, and are heart- or kidney-shaped. The cream to greenish-yellow flowers are somewhat bell-shaped, and grouped at the top of a tall, thin, leafless stem. The flowers have a decidedly hairy appearance.

The genus name, *Heuchera*, honours Johann Heinrich von Heucher, an 18th-century German botanist and physician. The species name, *cylindrica*, refers to the shape of the flowers. Alumroot was important for medicinal purposes for Native peoples. It works as a styptic for stopping bleeding and closing wounds. These plants are still used by herbalists. The root of the plant is a very intense astringent (like alum), thus the common name for the plant. Alumroot is also used as a mordant to fix dyes, and many people prefer it to the manufactured alternatives. This plant is sometimes called Sticky Alumroot, a reference to the sticky, glandular hairs on the upper stem.

Spotted Saxifrage
Saxifraga bronchialis

SAXIFRAGE FAMILY

These beautiful flowers inhabit rocky crevices, rock faces, screes, and open slopes, often appearing as if by magic from the rocks. The plant forms dense cushions that cover the ground. The white flowers appear in clusters at the top of the wiry brown stems, and have small red or yellow spots near the tips of the five petals. A close examination of this beautiful flower is well worth the time.

The origin of the genus name, *Saxifraga*, is explained in the note on Alaska Saxifrage (Rusty Saxifrage) (*S. ferruginea*), shown on page 210. The species name, *bronchialis*, is from the Latin *bronchus*, meaning "branch" or "division," a reference to the branching, mat-like growth of the plant. The plant is also known by the locally common name Yellow Dot Saxifrage.

Three-Toothed Mitrewort (Three-Parted Mitrewort)
Mitella trifida

SAXIFRAGE FAMILY

This grey-hairy perennial grows from a rhizome and occurs in moist forests at middle elevations. The plant is locally frequent on southern Vancouver Island and in southwestern British Columbia. The flowering stem is erect and grows up to 35 cm tall. The leaves are basal, nearly round with heart-shaped bases, long-stalked, and indistinctly lobed with five to seven lobes that may have rounded teeth on the margins. There are no leaves on the stem. The inflorescence is a spike-like cluster of 10 to 20 bell-shaped white flowers that have three elliptic lobes. The flowers are often held on one side of the hairy stem.

The origin of the genus name, *Mitella*, is explained in the narrative on Bishop's Cap (*M. nuda*), shown on page 211. The species name, *trifida*, means "cleft into three parts," a reference to the flower construction of the plant. Plants in the genus are usually referred to as Mitreworts. There are a number of Mitreworts in the region. A full catalogue of the various Mitreworts is outside the ambit of this book and specific identification may require further research. These plants are certainly among the most fascinating in the forest.

Woodland Star (Small-Flowered Woodland Star)
Lithophragma parviflorum

SAXIFRAGE FAMILY

This perennial grows up to 30 cm tall and occurs in low elevation grasslands, open ponderosa pine stands, and sagebrush areas. It blooms early in the spring. The leaves are mostly basal, kidney-shaped with deeply cleft and divided blades. The flowers are white to pinkish and occur in clusters at the tip of the stem. The flowers are broadly funnel shaped, with five spreading, deeply lobed petals.

The genus name, *Lithophragma*, is puzzling. It is derived from the Greek *lithos*, meaning "stone," and *phragma*, meaning "wall," suggesting a habitat different from that where the plant appears. Another common name for this plant is Fringe-Cup, referring to the deeply cleft petals, which are so deeply cleft that it almost appears as if the flower is fringed. This should not be confused with Fringe Cup (*Tellima grandiflora*), shown on page 213, which is a different species. Woodland Star flowers resemble Field Chickweed (*Cerastium arvense*), shown on page 193, but the petals of the former are notched in threes, where the latter are notched in twos.

Roundleaf Sundew
Drosera rotundifolia

SUNDEW FAMILY

This odd little plant lives in bogs, swamps, and fens, where it often forms colonies. It stands up to 25 cm tall and is insectivorous, meaning it eats insects, which are usually in no short supply in the plant's preferred habitat. The basal leaves are erect to ascending, have round blades on stalks up to 9 cm long, and have long reddish hairs along their margins, with each hair tipped with a sticky insect-trapping fluid. One authority describes the leaf blades as looking "like small green frying-pans." The flowers are small and white, and occur on one side only at the top of a naked flowering stem. The flowers open only in full sun. Insects are trapped in the sticky fluid on the leaves, then are digested by the plant as a source of nitrogen.

The genus name, *Drosera*, is derived from the Greek *droseros*, which means "dewy," a reference to the gland-tipped hairs on the leaves, the secretions of which make them appear moist. The species name, *rotundifolia*, refers to the leaf shape. A similar species, Narrow-Leaved Sundew (*D. anglica*) occurs in similar habitat, but its leaves are not round, and are several times longer than broad and are held upright on long stalks. *Drosera* are widespread in North America, Eurasia, and Australia.

Sitka Valerian
Valeriana sitchensis

VALERIAN FAMILY

This perennial grows up to 80 cm tall and has a somewhat succulent, squarish stem. It occurs in moist subalpine and alpine environments, in alpine meadows, and along streams. The leaves are large and opposite, divided into three to seven coarsely toothed lobes, with progressively shorter petioles up the stem. The numerous tubular flowers are crowded into a nearly flat-topped cluster at the top of the stem. The buds and young flowers are a pale lavender colour, but the flowers later fade to white. The floral tubes are notched into five equal lobes

There appear to be two schools of thought as to where this genus gets its name. One school opines that the genus name is from Valeria, a Roman province in southern Europe, now a part of Hungary. The other school contends that the genus name comes from the Latin *valere*, meaning "to be healthy," a reference to the fact that the plant has long been used for various medicinal purposes. The species name, *sitchensis*, is from Sitka Sound in southeastern Alaska, where the species was first collected and described. Two common names for the plant are Wild Heliotrope and Tobacco Root. The Tobacco Root Range in Montana takes its name from the plant. Valerian is the original source of diazepam, a tranquilizer and muscle relaxant commonly known as Valium.

Canada Violet
Viola canadensis

VIOLET FAMILY

This plant grows from short, thick rhizomes with slender creeping runners, and it favours moist to fairly dry deciduous forests, floodplains, and clearings. The flowers are held on aerial stems and are white with yellow bases. The lower three petals have purple pencilling and the upper two have a purplish tinge on back. The leaves are heart-shaped, long-stalked, decidedly pointed at the tip, and have saw-toothed edges. This small white flower splashes shady woods and marshes in the mid-summer.

The genus name, *Viola*, is derived from the Latin *violaceous*, a reference to the purple colour of many members of the genus. These violets are easily propagated from runners or sections of rhizomes, but can be invasive in a garden setting. Violet flowers have long been used as a poultice for swellings. Kidney-Leaved Violet (*V. renifolia*) is another white violet in the region. It has kidney-shaped leaves with round-tooth edges, and its flowers are borne on flowering stems that are shorter than the leave stalks.

Broad-Leaved Arrowhead (Wapato)
Sagittaria latifolia

WATER PLANTAIN FAMILY

Virginia Skilton image

This perennial is an aquatic plant that grows flowering stems up to 90 cm long from tubers and slender rhizomes in shallow ponds, lake-shores, marshes, slow-moving water, and ditches, from the prairies to the montane zone. The submerged leaves are simple, narrow, and tapered at both ends. The emergent leaves are distinctive. They are large (up to 25 cm long and 15 cm wide), with long stalks, and are decidedly arrowhead-shaped. The plant produces both male and female flowers, and they are different. The female flowers (pistillate) tend to develop first, and are ball-like clusters on small stalks, appearing lower on the plant than do the male flowers. The male flowers (staminate) are showy, with three broadly oval white petals, and numerous stamens. The male flowers appear on long stalks.

The genus name, *Sagittaria*, is derived from the Latin *sagitta*, which means "arrow," a reference to the shape of the emergent leaves, and the source of the common name. The species name, *latifolia*, means "broad-leaved." The tuber is described as resembling a walnut or golf ball. Wapato (sometimes spelled Wapatoo or Wappato) is the Chinook jargon trade language word for the tuber of this plant, which historically was a food and trade item. Native peoples gathered the tubers with digging sticks, or with bare toes moved around in the mud where the plants grew. Members of the Lewis and Clark Expedition ate the tubers while over-wintering on the Columbia River in 1805, and allowed that they tasted of roasted potatoes. Other common names applied to the plant include Duck Potato, Indian Potato, and Swamp Potato. Arumleaf Arrowhead (*S. cuneata*) is a similar species that occurs in similar habitat in the region. It has smaller leaves, flower stalks, and flowers.

Mist Maiden (Cliff Romanzoffia)
Romanzoffia sitchensis

WATERLEAF FAMILY

Dave Ingram image

This dainty, smooth, tufted perennial is fairly rare and occurs on moist rocky cliffs and ledges only in the subalpine and alpine zones. The leaves are mostly basal, kidney-shaped, and have five to nine lobes. The white to cream-coloured flowers are borne in loose clusters on thin stems above the leaves. The flowers are five-petalled and funnel-shaped at the base, each with a yellow eye.

The genus name, *Romanzoffia*, honours Count Nikolai Romanzoff, a 19th-century Russian patron of science who sponsored scientific explorations. Hooded Ladies' Tresses (*Spiranthes romanzoffiana*), shown on page 182, is also named in his honour. The species name, *sitchensis*, refers to Sitka Sound in southeastern Alaska, where the plant was first collected for science during an expedition sponsored by Count Romanzoff.

Silverleaf Phacelia (Scorpionweed)
Phacelia hastata

WATERLEAF FAMILY

This tap-rooted perennial grows up to 50 cm tall, and occurs from low to subalpine elevations in dry basins, gravelly areas, and roadsides. The leaves are elliptic with prominent veins, and generally are covered with silvery hairs. The flowers are white to lavender, funnel-shaped, and occur in compact clusters that spiral up the stem. The flowers have five broad petal lobes, five narrow hairy sepals, and five long stamens that extend well past the petals.

The origin of the genus name, *Phacelia*, is discussed in the note on Silky Phacelia (*P. sericea*), shown on page 106. The common name, Scorpionweed, arises because some people say the coiled branches of the flower clusters resemble the tail of a scorpion. The species is called Silverleaf because of the fine, silvery hairs on the leaves. The species name, *hastata*, is derived from the Latin *hastatus*, meaning "armed with a spear," a reference to the spearhead shape of some of the leaves.

Red, Orange, and Pink Flowers

This section contains flowers that are red,
orange, or pink when encountered in the field.
Flowers that are pinkish often can have tones
running to lavender, so if you do not find the
flower you are looking for, check the
other sections of this book.

Wild Ginger
Asarum caudatum

BIRTHWORT FAMILY

This plant is a low, creeping, matted perennial that appears in moist, shady woods at low to middle elevations. The plant is easily missed owing to its low-growing habit. The paired, opposite, glossy, evergreen leaves are kidney- to heart-shaped, 4–10 cm long and slightly wider, and are borne on long, hairy stalks. The flower nestles between the leaves, often hidden by them. The flower is purple-brown, solitary, and has three distinctive, long (3–8 cm), tapering petals. The plant exudes a faint odour of ginger, and is pollinated by flies, ants, millipedes, and other "creepy crawlers."

The genus name, *Asarum*, is derived from the Greek *asaron*, an Old World species. The species name, *caudatum*, is Latin for "tailed," a reference to the long, tapering petals on the flower. Native peoples used the plant for a variety of medicinal purposes. A tea was brewed from the root to treat colds, indigestion, and stomach pains, and the leaves were used in poultices applied to boils, skin infections, and toothaches. The plant is not related to the gingers used in Asian cuisine, which are in the genus *Zingiber*.

Falsebox
Paxistima myrsinites (formerly *Pachistima myrsinites*)

BITTERSWEET FAMILY

This dense evergreen shrub grows low to the ground or up to 60 cm tall at low to middle elevations in coniferous forests. The branches on the plant are reddish brown and exhibit four ridges. The leaves are opposite, glossy, leathery, and sharply toothed. The relatively inconspicuous flowers are tiny, brick red to maroon, cruciform-shaped with four petals, occurring in clusters along the branches in the leaf axils. The flowers bloom early in the year and are quite fragrant.

The genus name, *Paxistima*, is derived from the Greek *pachus*, meaning "thick," and *stigma*, a reference to the thick stigmas of the flowers on the plant. The species name, *myrsinites*, is derived from the Greek word for myrrh, the gum resin used in perfumes, medicine, and incense. This reference is undoubtedly to the fragrance of the flowers. The common name of the plant is derived from the Latin *buxus*, a "box" being a receptacle that was made from the boxwood tree, a tree that is reminiscent in form and foliage to this plant. The plant is also known as Mountain Boxwood, Oregon Boxwood, and Mountain-Lover. The branches from the plant are used extensively in the florist trade, even to the point of depleting the native stocks in places.

Common Hound's-Tongue
Cynoglossum officinale

BORAGE FAMILY

This coarse, hairy biennial weed was introduced from Europe and grows in disturbed ground and roadside ditches. It has a single leafy stem that grows up to 80 cm tall. The leaves are alternate, elliptic to lance-shaped, tapered to slender stalks at the base of the plant, and becoming stalkless and clasping near the top of the plant. The flowers are reddish-purple and funnel-shaped, with five spreading lobes. The flowers appear from the upper leaf axils. The fruits are clusters of small nutlets that are covered with barbed prickles.

The genus name, *Cynoglossum*, is derived from the Greek *cynos*, meaning "dog," and *glossa*, meaning "tongue." The hooked spines on the fruits catch on clothing and fur, a mechanism for seed distribution. Some people experience skin irritation when they come into contact with the plant. In the words of the famous naturalist Lewis J. Clark: "The plant is coarse and unattractive."

Mountain Sorrel
Oxyria digyna

BUCKWHEAT FAMILY

This relatively low-growing plant often appears in clumps in moist rocky areas, along streams, and at lake margins in the subalpine and alpine zones. The long-stalked leaves are often reddish, primarily basal, smooth with wavy margins, and are distinctively kidney- or heart-shaped. The flowers appear in crowded clusters along several upright stems. The flowers are relatively inconspicuous, tiny, and green to reddish. The fruits are flattened, papery, red seeds that have broad translucent wings.

The genus name, *Oxyria*, is derived from the Greek *oxys*, meaning "sour" or "sharp," a reference to the tart taste of the leaves. The common name, Sorrel, is said to originate from the Old High German word *sur*, meaning "sour." The plant is rich in vitamin C, and is said to be an antiscorbutic – a preventative for scurvy. A number of Native peoples used the plant as food. Mammals and birds also eat the plant.

Water Smartweed (Water Knotweed)
Polygonum amphibium

BUCKWHEAT FAMILY

This plant occurs from prairie to subalpine elevations, and is found in ponds, marshes, ditches, and lakeshores, often forming mats in standing water. The plant may grow on land adjacent to or in the water. The leaves are large, oblong to lance-shaped, rounded or pointed at the tips, and have a prominent midvein. The flowers are pink and occur in a dense, oblong cluster at the top of thick, smooth stalks.

The genus name, *Polygonum*, is derived from the Greek *poly*, meaning "many," and *gonu*, meaning "knee." The authorities differ on whether this refers to the contorted, many-jointed rootstock from which the plant grows, or to the numerous joints in the stems of the plants in this genus. The contorted shape of the rhizome is probably the source of the common name for many plants in the genus: Knotweed. The species name, *amphibium*, refers to the aquatic habitat of the plant. The plant was used by Native peoples both medicinally – in poultices to treat piles and skin disease – and as food. The plant is also food for a large variety of birds.

Red Columbine (Western Columbine)
Aquilegia formosa

BUTTERCUP FAMILY

These beautiful flowers are found in meadows and dry to moist woods, and are among the showiest of all western wildflowers. The leaves of the plant are mostly basal and compound, with three sets of three leaflets each. The flowers occur on stems above the basal leaves, and the stem leaves are smaller than the basal leaves, only appearing with three leaflets each. The five petals have red spurs above, and yellow blades below. The five sepals are red. Numerous stamens extend well beyond the petal blades.

The origin of the genus name, *Aquilegia*, is the subject of some debate. One school holds that it is from the Latin *aquila*, meaning "eagle," and is a reference to the long, talon-like spur on the flower. Another school argues that the genus name is from *aqua*, meaning "water," and *legere*, meaning "collect," a reference to the drops of nectar that gather at the ends of the spurs. The common name, Columbine, is derived from *columba*, meaning "dove," it being said that the petals resembled a group of doves drinking at a dish. An interesting juxtaposition, with the war symbol eagle in one camp, and the peace symbol dove in the other. The species name, *formosa*, means "comely" or "beautiful." The plant also goes by the locally common names of Western Columbine and Sitka Columbine. Bumblebees and butterflies favour Columbines. Where the range of this plant and Yellow Columbine (*A. flavescens*), shown on page 11, overlap, they may hybridize to produce flowers with pink tinged sepals.

Western Meadow Rue
Thalictrum occidentale

BUTTERCUP FAMILY

Western Meadow Rue is a dioecious species, which means that the male and female flowers are found on separate plants. The leaves on the plant are very similar in appearance to those of Columbines (*Aquilegia*), occurring in threes, but this plant's leaves are three times ternate – 3 x 3 x 3 – for a total of 27 leaflets per leaf. Neither gender of flowers has any petals. The male flower resembles a small wind chime, with the stamens hanging down like tassels. The female flowers resemble small star-shaped pinwheels. The plant prefers cool, moist forest environments.

The genus name, *Thalictrum*, is derived from the Greek *thallos*, which means "young shoot" or "green bough," a reference to the plant's bright green early shoots. The species name, *occidentale*, means "of the west." Native peoples used the plant variously as a medicine, a love charm, and a stimulant to horses. In modern times the plant is being investigated in chemotherapy research for cancer for its naturally occurring bioagents.

Windflower
Anemone multifida

BUTTERCUP FAMILY

This plant favours south-facing slopes, grasslands, and open woods. Like all anemones, Windflowers possess no petals, only sepals. The flowers are a variety of colours, from white, to yellowish, to red, and appear atop a woolly stem. Beneath the flowers are bract-like leaves attached directly to the stem. The leaves are palmate, with deeply incised, silky-haired leaflets, somewhat reminiscent of poppy leaves. The fruits are achenes in a rounded head, which later form a large cottony mass.

The common name, Windflower, comes from the method of distributing the long-plumed seeds of the plant. Some Native peoples burned the cottony seeds of the plant, using the resulting smoke as a remedy for headaches. This flower is also commonly referred to as Cut-Leaved Anemone and Pacific Anemone.

Bull Thistle
Cirsium vulgare

COMPOSITE FAMILY

This plant is a Eurasian weed that was introduced to North America and is common in pastures, waste places, clearings, and roadsides. The flowers are large composite heads with purple disk flowers and no ray flowers. The flower heads are bulbous and covered in sharp spikes. The flower structure is extraordinarily intricate when examined closely. The leaves, both basal and stem, are lance-shaped, deeply lobed, and spiny, clasping the stem. The Bull Thistle will grow to over 2 m tall, and will produce a multitude of flowers.

There is some dispute among the authorities as to the origin of the genus name, *Cirsium*. One school argues that the name originates from the Greek *kirsos*, which means "swollen vein," a condition that these plants were once said to heal. The other school opines that the genus name, is derived from the Latin *circum*, which means "around," possibly a reference to the fact that many members of the genus have spikes on the entire rounded surface of the flower heads. All thistles have spines on their leaf edges, but the Bull Thistle is the only one with a spiny leaf surface. The flowers are a favourite of bees and butterflies. The thistle generally is the national emblem of Scotland, legend having it that a soldier in an invading Danish army stepped on a thistle and cried out in pain, awaking and alerting the Scottish encampment, who rose and repelled the invading army. The thistle was thereafter considered to be the guardian of Scotland. Bull Thistle is also known locally as Spear Thistle.

Canada Thistle
Cirsium arvense

COMPOSITE FAMILY

Despite the common name, this noxious weed was introduced to North America from Eurasia. The plant grows to over 1 m tall from a thin, white, creeping rhizome. The flowers occur in heads at the tops of the multiple branches. The flowers are usually pinkish to mauve, but they may be white. The leaves are alternate and oblong to lance-shaped, with wavy margins.

The origin of the genus name, *Cirsium*, is explained in the narrative on Bull Thistle (*C. vulgare*), shown on page 235. The species name, *arvense*, means "of cultivated fields," and the plant certainly lives up to its name. By combining a creeping rhizome and tremendous seed distribution, the plant will quickly take over areas where it grows. If the rhizome is cut or broken by farm machinery, the spread of the plant is exacerbated. Canada Thistle is dioecious – that is, male and female flowers occur on separate plants.

Common Burdock
Arctium minus

COMPOSITE FAMILY

A plant of pastures, roadsides, fencerows, and disturbed sites, Common Burdock is erect with spreading branches, and grows to over 1 m tall. The flowers appear at the ends of the branches as purplish to pinkish tubular protrusions with disk florets only. The outer bracts are decidedly hooked at the ends and form a ball around the inflorescence, making the plant appear to be furry and unkempt.

Arctium species are native to and widespread in Eurasia. In Japan the edible roots of the plants are known as *gobo*. It is said that the hooks on the involucral bracts of this plant inspired the creation of Velcro. These hooks are extraordinarily efficient in disseminating the seeds of the plant, clinging as they do to fur on animals and clothing on humans who encounter the plant in the field.

Orange Agoseris (Orange-Flowered False Dandelion)
Agoseris aurantiaca

COMPOSITE FAMILY

This is a common plant in moist to dry openings, meadows, and dry open forests in mid to alpine elevations. The plant is also known as False Dandelion, and occurs in both yellow, known as Pale Agoseris (*A. glauca*), and orange. Agoseris shares many characteristics with the Dandelion (*Taraxacum officinale*), shown on page 19, including a long taproot, a rosette of basal leaves, a leafless stem, a single flower appearing on a long stalk, and the production of a sticky, milky juice that is apparent when the stem is broken. Agoseris is generally a taller plant than Dandelion, its leaves are longer, and the leaf blades are smooth or faintly toothed rather than deeply incised as Dandelion's are. The bracts of the Agoseris flower heads are broader than Dandelion, and are never turned back along the stem as they are in Dandelion.

The genus name, *Agoseris*, is the Greek name for an allied Old World plant. The species name, *aurantiaca*, means "orange." Some Native peoples used the milky juice of the plant as a chewing gum. Infusions from the plant were also used for a variety of medicinal purposes.

Orange Hawkweed
Hieracium aurantiacum

COMPOSITE FAMILY

A plant common to open woods, meadows, roadsides, ditches, and disturbed areas from low to subalpine areas, this conspicuous flower is an introduced species from Europe, where it has long been a garden ornamental. The species can spread rapidly and become a noxious weed. Indeed, one common name applied to the plant is Orange-Red King Devil. The orange flower heads appear in a cluster on ascending stalks. The flowers are composed entirely of ray florets; there are no disk florets. The leaves are broadly lance- to spoon-shaped, in a basal rosette.

The genus name, *Hieracium,* is derived from the Greek *hierax,* which means "hawk," as it was once believed that eating these plants improved a hawk's vision. The species name, *aurantiacum,* means "orange coloured." The leaves, stems, and roots produce a milky latex that was used as a chewing gum by British Columbia tribes. A white-flowered form of Hawkweed (*H. albiflorum*) also appears in the region in open woods, but its white flowers appear singly at the tops of many-branched stems, not as clusters.

Pink Pussytoes
Antennaria rosea

COMPOSITE FAMILY

This mat-forming species is a low perennial that spreads by trailing stems, and occurs from valley floors to the subalpine zone. The leaves are spatula-shaped, and grey-hairy on both surfaces. The basal leaves are larger than those on the slender stem of the plant. The flower heads are composed entirely of disk florets that are pinkish. The flower heads are surrounded by several thin, translucent, overlapping bracts.

In the *Antennaria* genus, the male and female flowers are on separate plants. The genus name is derived from the Latin *antenna*, the reference being that the male flowers have parts that resemble the antennae of an insect. The soft, fuzzy flower heads of this genus give it the common name – Pussytoes – and a number of species occur in the same general habitat. The species name, *rosea*, refers to the colour of the flower heads.

Spotted Knapweed
Centaurea maculosa

COMPOSITE FAMILY

This introduced noxious weed inhabits roadsides, ditches, and disturbed areas, and has become a problem in many locales. The plant is many-branched and grows up to over a metre tall from creeping rhizomes. The flowers are heads at the ends of branches, with dark pink or purple disk florets only.

The name Knapweed is derived from the ancient English *knap*, meaning "knob" or "bump," a reference to the bumps on the branches of the plant. The genus name, *Centaurea*, is derived from the Greek *kentaur*, the mythical beast believed to have healing powers. The species name, *maculosa*, means "spotted," a reference to the spots on the bracts of the flowers. It is believed that this plant was inadvertently introduced into North America when its seeds contaminated a shipment of forage crop seeds. Another invasive relative, Diffuse Knapweed (*C. diffusa*), is also present in the region. It has cream-coloured flowers.

Black Gooseberry (Swamp Currant)
Ribes lacustre

CURRANT FAMILY

This is an erect deciduous shrub, growing up to 1.5 m tall, that occurs in moist woods and open areas from foothills to the subalpine zone. The branches of the plant have small prickles and stout thorns at leaf and branch bases. The leaves are alternate and shaped like maple leaves, with three to five deeply cleft, palmate lobes. The flowers are reddish, saucer-shaped, and hang in elongated clusters. The fruits are dark purple to black berries, which bristle with tiny hairs.

The genus name, *Ribes*, is derived from the Arabic *ribas*, the Moorish medical name for an unrelated rhubarb-like plant that grows in North Africa and Spain. The species name, *lacustre*, is derived from the Latin *lacus*, meaning "lake," or *lacustris*, meaning "inhabiting lakes." The genus includes all of the Currants and Gooseberries. This plant is also known as Bristly Black Currant and Black Swamp Gooseberry. Commonly, members of the *Ribes* genus are divided into Currants and Gooseberries depending upon whether or not the berries are bristly hairy – Currants are not bristly hairy, and Gooseberries are. The spines on the plant can cause allergic reactions in some people.

Flowering Red Currant (Red-Flower Currant)
Ribes sanguineum

CURRANT FAMILY

This early-blooming plant is an upright shrub that grows to 3 m tall in open, dry woods, along roadsides, and in logged areas from low to middle elevations. It has reddish-brown bark, and the leaves are triangular, deeply three-lobed, toothed and up to 6 cm wide. The flowers are numerous, rose-red to pink, tubular with five spreading lobes, and occur in clusters, with 10 to 20 flowers blooming together. The unpalatable fruit is round, black and often covered with a blue bloom.

The origin of the genus name, *Ribes*, is discussed in the note on Black Gooseberry (*R. lacustre*), shown on page 242. All of the currants and gooseberries are in this genus. The species name, *sanguineum*, means "blood red," a reference to the inflorescence of the plant. This plant has been used extensively as a garden ornamental. Indeed, in 1827 the redoubtable explorer and plant collector David Douglas (namesake of the Douglas fir) carried seeds for Flowering Red Currant back to England and sold them, making sufficient funds on the sale to recover the entire cost of his just-ended two-year expedition.

Spreading Dogbane
Apocynum androsaemifolium

DOGBANE FAMILY

A fairly common shrub in thickets and wooded areas, this plant has freely branching, slender stems. The leaves are opposite, egg-shaped, and have sharp-pointed tips. The leaves generally droop during the heat of the day. The small, bell-shaped, pink flowers droop from the ends of the leafy stems, usually in clusters. The petal lobes are spreading and bent back, usually with dark pink veins.

The genus name, *Apocynum*, is derived from the Greek *apo*, meaning "against," and *kyon*, meaning "dogs," thus the common name. The pods of the plant are poisonous and it may have been that the pods were used to concoct a poison for dispensing with unwanted dogs. The tough fibres from the stems of Dogbanes were rolled into a strong, fine thread by Native peoples. Several strands plaited together were used for bow strings, and the cord was also used to make fishing nets. When broken, the leaves and stems exude a milky sap. The plant contains a chemical related to the heart disease drug called digitalis, and was once used as a digitalis substitute, but harmful side effects brought an end to that practice. A similar species, Indian-Hemp Dogbane (*A. cannabinum*) occurs in similar habitat, but it is a generally larger species with small flowers and ascending leaves. The two species can overlap and interbreed, producing an intermediate species known as Western Dogbane (*A. medium*).

Fireweed (Great Willowherb)
Epilobium angustifolium

EVENING PRIMROSE FAMILY

A plant of disturbed areas, roadsides, clearings and shaded woods that occurs from low elevations to the subalpine zone. This plant is often one of the first plants to appear after a fire. The pink, four-petalled flowers bloom in long terminal clusters. Bracts between the petals are narrow. The flowers bloom from the bottom of the cluster first, then upward on the stem. The leaves are alternate and appear whorled.

The genus name, *Epilobium*, is derived from the Greek *epi*, meaning "upon," and *lobos*, meaning "a pod," a reference to the inflorescence of plants of this genus occurring on top of the seed pod. The species name, *angustifolium*, means "narrow-leafed." The common name originates from the plant's tendency to spring up from seeds and rhizomes on burned-over lands. The leaves resemble willow leaves, hence the alternative common name Willowherb. The young leaves can be used in salads, and a weak tea can be brewed from the plant. The inner pith can be used to thicken soups and stews. Fireweed is the floral emblem of the Yukon. A related species, Purple-Leaved Willowherb (*E. ciliatum*) also occurs in the region. It has small pink to white to rose-coloured flowers that appear in a cluster at the top of the stem.

River Beauty (Broad-Leaved Willowherb)
Epilobium latifolium

EVENING PRIMROSE FAMILY

Also known as Dwarf Fireweed, this plant grows as a pioneer, often in dense colonies, on gravelly floodplains, and river bars, where the dense leaves and waving pink to purple flowers often obscure the stony ground underneath. River Beauty strongly resembles common Fireweed (*E. angustifolium*), shown on page 245, in appearance, but it has much shorter stems, broader leaves, and larger, more brilliantly coloured flowers. The large and showy, pink to rose-purple, four-petalled flowers bloom in a loose, short, leafy inflorescence. The leaves are bluish-green and waxy, with rounded tips.

The origin of the genus name, *Epilobium*, is explained in the narrative on Fireweed. The species name, *latifolium*, means "broad-leaved." Plants in this genus are also known by the locally common name of Willowherb. This plant is also locally known as Broad-Leaved Willowherb and Mountain Fireweed. The plant is cooling and astringent, and was used by some Native peoples to promote healing of wounds. Another related species, Alpine Willowherb (*E. anagallidifolium*) occurs in the area. That species is a low, mat-forming plant that appears in moist to wet rocky areas in the subalpine and alpine zones. The flowers are tiny, and may be pink to rose-coloured to white.

Elephant's Head
Pedicularis groenlandica

FIGWORT FAMILY

This is a plant of wet meadows, stream banks, and wetland margins. The flowers appear in dense clusters atop a substantial stalk which can grow to 50 cm tall. Each of the flowers is reddish-purple to pinkish, and has an uncanny resemblance to an elephant's head, with a curved trunk and flared ears.

The origin of the genus name, *Pedicularis*, is explained in the narrative on Bracted Lousewort (*P. bracteosa*), shown on page 32. The species name, *groenlandica*, means "Greenland," though the learned references all seem to be in accord that the first specimens of the plant were found in Labrador, and nobody seems able to explain how Greenland got into the picture. All members of the genus are somewhat parasitic on the roots of other plants, so transplantation is doomed to failure. When encountered, a close examination of this delightful flower is recommended, but be careful of the fragile habitat in which it lives. The plant also goes by the locally common names Little Elephant Head and Elephant's Head Lousewort.

Red Monkeyflower (Lewis's Monkeyflower)
Mimulus lewisii

FIGWORT FAMILY

This plant occurs, often in large patches, along mountain streams, and other moist areas in the subalpine and alpine zones. The leaves are clasping, opposite, conspicuously veined, and have irregular teeth along the margins. The showy red flowers arise from the axils of the upper leaves. The corolla is funnel-shaped and has two lips. The upper lip is two-lobed and often bent backward, and the lower lip is three-lobed, with hairs in the throat and yellow markings on the lobes.

The origin of the genus name, *Mimulus*, is discussed in the note on Yellow Monkeyflower (*M. guttatus*), shown on page 35. The species name, *lewisii*, is in honour of Meriwether Lewis of the Lewis and Clark Expedition, who collected the first specimen of the plant in 1805 near the headwaters of the Missouri River in what is now the State of Montana. Hummingbirds and bees are attracted to these flowers.

Red Paintbrush
Castilleja miniata

FIGWORT FAMILY

A plant of alpine meadows, well-drained slopes, open subalpine forests, moist stream banks, and open foothills woods, Paintbrush is widely distributed and extremely variable in colour. The leaves are narrow and sharp-pointed, linear to lance-shaped, usually without teeth or divisions, but sometimes the upper leaves have three shallow lobes. The showy red, leafy bracts, which are actually modified leaves, resemble a brush dipped in paint, hence the common name.

The genus name, *Castilleja*, commemorates Domingo Castillejo, an 18th-century Spanish botanist. The species name, *miniata*, refers to the scarlet-red colour minium, an oxide of lead. There are a number of species of Paintbrush in the region and they vary enormously in colour – from pink, to red, to yellow, to white – but their general appearance is distinctive and recognizable, regardless of colour. Some of the colour variations are shown on the next page. Specific identification is outside the ambit of this volume, and if you wish more specific identifications I encourage consultation with other authorities. Although beautiful, this plant should not be transplanted, as it is partially parasitic and does not survive transplanting.

Paintbrush Colour Variations

Thin-Leaved Owl's Clover
Orthocarpus tenuifolius

FIGWORT FAMILY

This plant grows up to 30 cm tall at low to subalpine elevations in dry grasslands and forests. The leaves are alternate, linear, unstalked, and up to 5 cm long. The inflorescence is a dense, prominently bracted terminal spike. The petal-like bracts are broad, blunt tipped, and pinkish-purple. Owl's Clovers are very similar to the Paintbrushes (*Castillejas*), but the latter are mostly perennial, while the Owl's Clovers are annuals. In addition, the Paintbrushes have an upper floral lip that is much longer than the lower lip. In the Owl's Clovers, the upper floral lip is only slightly longer than the lower lip, if at all.

The genus name, *Orthocarpus*, is derived from the Greek *orthos*, meaning "straight," and *karpos*, which means "fruit," a reference to the seed capsule of the plant. The first botanical specimen of the plant was collected in 1806 by Meriwether Lewis on the banks of Clark's River (now known as the Bitterroot River) while camped at a place called Travelers Rest in present-day Montana. The Lewis and Clark party rested there after the exhausting crossing of the Bitterroot Mountains on their return from the Pacific.

Strawberry Blite
Chenopodium capitatum

GOOSEFOOT FAMILY

This plant is found from valley to subalpine elevations, and is distinctive for its large triangular or arrowhead-shaped leaves and its dense, fleshy clusters of bright red flowers. The flower clusters appear at the ends of branches on the plant, usually in interrupted bunches, and in the leaf axils.

The genus name, *Chenopodium*, is Greek for "goose foot," a reference to the leaf's resemblance to the foot of a goose. The leaves are rich in vitamins and minerals, and are said to taste like spinach. The flowers are also edible, though most authorities warn against over-indulging in consuming the plant. Some Native peoples used the red flowers as a source of dye, it being bright red initially, then darkening to purple as it ages. Another common name for the plant is Indian Paint.

Bearberry (Kinnikinnick)
Arctostaphylos uva-ursi

HEATH FAMILY

This trailing or matted evergreen shrub grows low to the ground, and has long branches with reddish, flaky bark and shiny green, leathery leaves. The flowers are pale pink and urn-shaped, appearing in clumps at the ends of the stems. The fruits are dull red berries.

The genus name, *Arctostaphylos*, is derived from the Greek *arktos*, meaning "bear," and *staphyle*, meaning "bunch of grapes." The species name, *uva-ursi*, is Latin for "bear's grape." The berries are apparently relished by bears and birds, though they tend to be dry and mealy to humans. They are edible and have been used as food, prepared in a variety of ways. The berries remain on the plant through the winter. One of the common names, Kinnikinnick, is believed to be of Algonquin origin, and means "something to smoke," a reference to the fact that some Native peoples used the leaves of the plant as a tobacco.

Black Huckleberry (Thinleaf Huckleberry)
Vaccinium membranaceum

HEATH FAMILY

Doug Skilton image

This erect, densely branched, deciduous shrub grows up to 1.5 m tall at middle to high elevations in dry to moist coniferous forests. The leaves are lance-shaped to elliptic, with pointed tips and finely toothed margins. The leaves turn red or purple in the fall. The flowers are creamy pink and urn-shaped, nodding on slender stalks. The fruits are black to dark purple berries, 8–10 mm across.

Without question, the berry of this plant is among the most sought-after wild berries that occur in the mountains – by human consumers, birds and bears. The sweet taste of the berry is distinctive, and the berries are used to make jams, syrups and liqueurs. Among those who harvest the berries, picking sites are jealously guarded. My son once asked a picker where he found the berries. The picker answered: "Sonny, I would sooner tell you I was sleeping with your wife than I would where I pick Huckleberries!" A similar species, Red Huckleberry (*V. parvifolium*), occurs in the region, but it has pinkish-yellow flowers and produces a bright red berry.

Bog Cranberry
Vaccinium oxycoccos (also *Oxycoccus oxycoccus*)

HEATH FAMILY

This plant is a creeping, vine-like, dwarf evergreen shrub that grows up to 40 cm tall in bogs and in wet sphagnum moss, from low to subalpine elevations. The stems are thin, wiry and slightly hairy. The small leaves are alternate, leathery, sharp-pointed, and widely spaced on the stem. The leaves are dark green on the upper surface, lighter underneath, and the margins curl under. The nodding flowers are deep pink, with four petals that curve backward exposing the stamens, reminiscent of the shape of Shooting Star (*Dodecatheon pulchellum*), shown on page 101. The fruits are round red berries that appear disproportionately large for the tiny stems on which they hang.

The genus name, *Vaccinium*, is the Latin name for Blueberry. The species name, *oxycoccos*, is derived from the Greek *oxys*, meaning "acid, sharp or bitter," and *kokkos*, meaning "round berry," a reference to the tart taste of the fruits. The berries are rich in vitamin C, and were used by Native peoples as a food. Another so-called Cranberry appears in the area – the Low-Bush Cranberry (*Viburnum edule*), shown on page 158 – but it is a member of the Honeysuckle Family, and is a substantially different plant. Another plant found in the region, Lingonberry (*V. vitis-idaea*), shown on page 150, is also commonly known as Bog Cranberry, but it has larger, leathery leaves and white to pinkish urn-shaped flowers.

False Azalea (Fool's Huckleberry)
Menziesia ferruginea

HEATH FAMILY

This deciduous shrub is erect and spreading, and grows up to 2 m tall
in moist, wooded sites in the foothills to subalpine zones. The twigs of the
shrub have fine, rust-coloured, sticky, glandular hairs, and give off a skunky
odour when crushed. The leaves are alternate, elliptic, and broader above the
middle. They are grey-hairy and have a prominent midvein protruding at
the tip. The flowers are small, pinkish to greenish-orange, urn-shaped, and
nodding on long, slender stalks. The flowers occur in clusters at the base of
new growth. The fruit is a dark purplish capsule.

The genus name, *Menziesia*, honours Archibald Menzies, a physician and
botanist who accompanied Captain George Vancouver in his northwest
explorations in the late 18th century. The species name, *ferruginea*, is Latin
meaning "iron rust," a reference to the rusty glands that cover the branches
and the leaves. In the fall the leaves of the shrub take on very attractive orange
and crimson colours. The common name False Azalea arises because the
leaves of this plant resemble those of garden Azaleas. Another common name
for the plant is Fool's Huckleberry, because the flowers might be mistaken for
those of Huckleberries.

Grouseberry
Vaccinium scoparium

HEATH FAMILY

This low deciduous shrub grows up to 20 cm tall and often forms dense ground cover on slopes in the foothills to subalpine zone. The branches are numerous, slender, and erect. The leaves are alternate, ovate, widest in the middle and sharp-pointed, with finely serrated margins. The flowers are small, pinkish, urn-shaped and nodding, hanging down singly from the leaf axils. The fruits are tiny, edible, bright red berries.

The Grouseberry is a member of the same genus as Blueberries, Huckleberries, and Cranberries. The species name, *scoparium*, is derived from the Latin *scopula*, meaning "broom-twig," a reference to the close, twiggy stems on the plant. The berries are very small, and some Native peoples gathered them using combs. Small mammals and birds eat the berries. Grouse eat all parts of the shrub, thus the common name Grouseberry. An allied species, Dwarf Blueberry (*V. caespitosum*), appears in similar habitat. It is a matting plant with reddish twigs, and it also has five-lobed, bell-shaped flowers that are borne singly from the leaf axils. Its fruits are small, blue, edible berries. Grouseberry also is known as Grouse Whortleberry. Whortleberry is a name applied in Europe to Bilberry, an Old World Blueberry.

Oval-Leaved Blueberry
Vaccinium ovalifolium

HEATH FAMILY

This deciduous shrub grows to over 2 m tall in moist to wet coniferous forests, clearings, and bogs at low to subalpine elevations. The pale pink flowers are urn-shaped, and appear singly at the leaf bases. The flowers may precede the arrival of the leaves. The berries are blue-black, dusted with a pale bluish bloom. The berries are somewhat large for wild blueberries, and have a pleasant flavour. The leaves are oval, blunt, and rounded at the ends, and usually lack teeth on the margins.

The origin of the genus name, *Vaccinium*, is discussed in the note on Bog Cranberry (*V. oxycoccos*), shown on page 255. The genus includes all of the wild Blueberries, Cranberries, and Huckleberries. The species name, *ovalifolium*, refers to the shape of the leaves. Another common name applied to this plant is Blue Huckleberry. Velvet-Leaved Blueberry (*V. myrtilloides*) is a similar species that occurs in the region. It is a low shrub, growing only 40 cm tall, and its leaves are softly hairy and elliptic to oblong with sharply pointed tips. It has cylindrically bell-shaped greenish-white flowers that occur singly or in clusters at the branch tips. Its berries are also very flavourful.

Pine-Drops
Pterospora andromedea

HEATH FAMILY

This purple or reddish-brown saprophyte (a plant that gets its nutrients from decaying plant or animal matter) stands up to a metre tall or more, and lives in deep humus of coniferous or mixed woods. The plants grow singly or in clusters, but they are rare. The leaves are mostly basal, and resemble scales. The stem stands erect, and is covered with glandular hairs. The flowers are cream-coloured to yellowish, and occur in a raceme that covers roughly the top half of the stalk. The petals are united into an urn shape, and hang downward off bent flower stalks, like small lanterns. The stalks of the plant will remain erect for a year or more after the plant dies.

The genus name, *Pterospora*, is derived from the Greek *pteron*, meaning "wing," and *sporos*, meaning "seed," a reference to the winged appearance of the seeds. The species name, *andromedea*, refers to Andromeda of Greek mythology. To review the story of Andromeda, see White Heather (*Cassiope mertensiana*), shown on page 155. I am at a complete loss as to how the taxonomist connected this plant to that particular myth, and I have so far been unable to explain the connection.

Pink Wintergreen
Pyrola asarifolia

HEATH FAMILY

This plant is an erect perennial that inhabits moist to dry coniferous and mixed forests, and riverine environments, from the montane to the subalpine zone. The flowers are shaped like an inverted cup or bell, nodding, waxy, pale pink to purplish red, and have a long, curved, projecting style. The leaves are basal in a rosette. The leaves have a leathery appearance, and are shiny, rounded, and dark green.

The origin of the genus name, *Pyrola*, is explained in the narrative on Greenish-Flowered Wintergreen (*P. chlorantha*), shown on page 147. The species name, *asarifolia*, is derived from the Latin *asarum*, meaning "ginger," and *folium*, meaning "leaf," a reference to the similarity between the leaves of this plant and those of wild ginger. Members of the genus contain salicylic acid, a compound very like the active ingredient in aspirin. In fact, the compound was originally isolated from the bark of willows, which are in the genus *Salix*. Two other species of *Pyrola*, Greenish-Flowered Wintergreen and One-Sided Wintergreen (*P. secunda*), shown on page 151, occur in similar habitat.

Pipsissewa (Prince's-Pine)
Chimaphila umbellata

HEATH FAMILY

This small evergreen shrub grows to 30 cm tall in coniferous woods. The dark green, glossy leaves are narrowly spoon-shaped, saw-toothed, and occur in whorls. The flowers are pink, waxy, saucer-shaped, and nodding on an erect stem above the leaves. The fruits of the plant are dry, round, brown capsules that often overwinter on the stem.

The genus name, *Chimaphila*, is derived from the Greek *cheima*, meaning "winter," and *philos*, meaning "loving," descriptive of the evergreen leaves. Pipsissewa is an adaptation of the Cree name for the plant, *pipsisikweu*, meaning "it breaks into small pieces," a reference to a substance in the leaves that was said to dissolve kidney and gall stones. The plant was often used to make a medicinal tea. Both Native peoples and settlers to North America used the plant for a variety of medicinal purposes. A related species, Little Prince's Pine (*C. menziesii*), occurs but rarely in the southeast of the region. It is a much smaller plant, seldom reaching more than 10 cm, and it has between one and three flesh-coloured flowers.

Red Heather (Pink Mountain Heather)
Phyllodoce empetriformis

HEATH FAMILY

This dwarf evergreen shrub grows up to 30 cm tall, and thrives in sub-alpine and alpine meadows and slopes near timberline. The leaves are blunt, needle-like, and grooved on both sides. The red to pink, urn-shaped flowers are erect and/or nodding in clusters at the top of the stems.

The genus name, *Phyllodoce*, appears to honour a sea nymph from Greek mythology, but none of the learned authorities seem to know why that mythical character is associated with this genus. The species name, *empetriformis*, also is a source of controversy. Some authorities say the name arises because the leaves of this plant resemble those of the genus *Empetrum* – the Crowberry Family. Other authorities say the species name is derived from the Greek *en*, meaning "on," and *petros*, meaning "rocks," a reference to the rocky habitat favoured by the plant. The plant is not a true heather. The first sample of it was collected by Lewis and Clark during their expedition, but the exact location of its collection has been lost. Yellow Heather (*P. glanduliflora*) is a similar plant that occurs in the same habitat as this species. It has yellowish-green flowers and very sticky glandular hairs. The two species often occur together and will easily hybridize.

Swamp Laurel (Western Bog Laurel)
Kalmia microphylla

HEATH FAMILY

This low-growing evergreen shrub occurs in cool bogs, on stream banks, and lakeshores in the subalpine and alpine zones. The leaves are leathery, dark green above and greyish-white beneath, often with the margins rolled under. The flowers are pink to rose-coloured, with the petals fused together to form a saucer or bowl, appearing on a reddish stalk. There are ten purple-tipped stamens protruding from the petals.

The genus name, *Kalmia*, is to honour Peter Kalm, a student of Carolus Linnaeus at Uppsala University in Sweden. Linnaeus was a prominent botanist who developed binomial nomenclature for plants. The species name, *microphylla*, means "small-leaved." The leaves and flowers of this plant contain poisonous alkaloids that can be fatal to humans and livestock if ingested.

Orange Honeysuckle (Western Trumpet)
Lonicera ciliosa

HONEYSUCKLE FAMILY

This is a climbing vine up to 6 m long that clambers over trees and shrubs in woodlands and forest openings from low to high elevations. It seems to prefer to climb on conifers. The leaves are broadly elliptic, up to 10 cm long, opposite on the stem, except the uppermost pair, which are connate – fused at their bases to form a shallow cup – and hairy on the margins. The flowers are vividly orange, tubular, up to 4 cm long, and appear in clusters of 5 to 25 blooms from inside the connate leaves. Unlike many members of the genus, these flowers have no scent.

The origin of the genus name, *Lonicera*, is discussed in the note on Black Twinberry (*L. involucrata*), shown on page 39. The species name, *ciliosa*, refers to the hairs on the margins of the connate leaves. This plant is also known by the locally common name Western Trumpet. Purple Honeysuckle (*L. hispidula*), is a related species that appears in similar habitat. It has a cluster of wine-purple flowers in its connate leaves. Native peoples used the stems of honeysuckles to fashion woven mats, bags, baskets, and blankets.

Snowberry
Symphoricarpos albus

HONEYSUCKLE FAMILY

This common deciduous shrub occurs from coast to coast in North America, and is found from prairies to lower subalpine zones, in well-drained, open or wooded sites. There are several subspecies that are so alike it requires dissection and magnification to tell one from the other. The shrub is erect, and grows up to 2 m tall. The branches are opposite and slender, and on close examination are seen to be covered with tiny hairs. The leaves are opposite, elliptic to oval, and pale green. The flowers are pink to white and broadly funnel-shaped, occurring in clusters at the ends of the twigs. The stamens and style do not protrude from the flower. The fruits are waxy, white berry-like drupes that occur in clusters, and often persist through the winter.

The genus name, *Symphoricarpos*, is derived from the Greek *symphorein*, which means "borne together," and *karpos*, which means "fruit," a reference to the clustered berries of the plant. The berries of this plant were not eaten by Native peoples, and many considered them poisonous. In fact, some Indians called the berries Corpse Berries and Ghost Berries. Some Native peoples believed that these white berries were the ghosts of Saskatoon berries, and thus part of the spirit world and not to be tampered with by the living.

Twinflower
Linnaea borealis

HONEYSUCKLE FAMILY

This small, trailing evergreen is common in coniferous forests, but easily overlooked by the casual observer. This plant sends runners creeping over the forest floor, over mosses, fallen logs, and stumps. At frequent intervals the runners give rise to the distinctive Y-shaped stems, 5–10 cm tall. Each fork of the stem supports at its end a slightly flared, pink-tinged to white, trumpet-like flower that hangs down like a small lantern on a tiny lamppost. The flowers have a sweet perfume that is most evident near evening.

The genus name, *Linnaea*, honours Carolus Linnaeus, the Swedish botanist who is the father of modern plant nomenclature. It is said that this flower was his favourite among the thousands of plants he knew. The species name, *borealis*, means "northern," referring to the circumpolar northern habitat of the plant. Some Native peoples made a tea from the leaves of this plant.

Columbia Lily (Tiger Lily)
Lilium columbianum

LILY FAMILY

True lilies are recognized by their large, showy flowers, smooth, unbranched stems, and whorls of narrow, lance-shaped leaves. Columbia Lily can have up to 30 flowers per stem. The orange to orange-yellow flowers are downward-hanging, with curled-back petals and deep red to purplish spots near the centre. The flowers are very similar to Western Wood Lily (*L. philadelphicum*), the floral emblem of the Province of Saskatchewan, shown on page 270, but the Wood Lily petals form more of a chalice shape, without the petals curling back like those of this species.

The common name, Tiger Lily, most probably comes from the spotting on the petals. There was once a superstition that smelling this species would give you freckles. The bulbs of the plants were used as food by Native tribes. They were said to have a peppery taste, and would add a peppery taste to other foods. Like many other lilies, this one will die if the flower is picked. The bulb depends upon the flower for nutrients, and if the flower is removed, the bulb will starve and die.

Nodding Onion
Allium cernuum

LILY FAMILY

All *Allium* species smell strongly of onion, and have small flower clusters at the top of the leafless stalk. Nodding Onion is a common species in the region, and is easily identified by its pink drooping or nodding inflorescence. There are usually 8 to 12 flowers in the nodding cluster.

Allium is the Latin name for "garlic," from the Celtic *all*, meaning "hot" or "burning," because it irritates the eyes. The species name, *cernuum*, refers to the crook in the stem of the plant just below the flower. The stem gives off an oniony odour when crushed, and is said to be one of the better tasting wild onions. Native peoples gathered the bulbs and ate them raw and cooked; used them for flavouring other foods; and dried them for later use. Ground squirrels also use this plant in their diets.

Sagebrush Mariposa Lily
Calochortus macrocarpus

LILY FAMILY

This is a large lily that occurs in the region in dry grasslands and open Ponderosa forests. It is similar to Three Spot Mariposa Lily (*C. apiculatus*), shown on page 171, but its pinkish to purplish petals are more pointed, and the gland at the base of each petal is a crescent-shaped. This plant grows in more arid environments, and blooms later than the Three Spot Mariposa Lily.

The origin of the common name, Mariposa, and the genus name, *Calochortus*, is discussed in the note on Three Spot Mariposa Lily. The species name, *macrocarpus* means "large seed." Like many other lilies, picking the flower of this plant will kill the plant because picking the flower deprives the bulb of needed nourishment. The range of this plant has been severely restricted over the years by grazing cattle. The plant will not accept transplantation, so it is best to enjoy it in the wild where it grows.

Western Wood Lily
Lilium philadelphicum (also *L. umbellatum*)

LILY FAMILY

This lily grows in moist meadows, dense to open woods, and edges of aspen groves, from prairie elevations to the low subalpine zone. The leaves are numerous, lance-shaped, smooth, and alternate on the stem, except for the upper leaves, which are in whorls. Each plant may produce from one to five bright orange to orange-red flowers, each with three petals and three similar sepals. The petals and the sepals are orange at the tip, becoming yellowish and black, or purple-dotted, at the bases. The anthers are dark purple in colour.

Lilium is the Latin name for the plant. There are several stories as to how the species name originates. One explanation holds that Linnaeus – the Swedish naturalist who invented binominal identification for plants – received his specimens of the plant from a student in Philadelphia. Another explanation holds that the name comes from the Greek words *philos*, meaning "love," and *delphicus*, the ancient wooded oracle at Delphi, hence "wood lover." The Western Wood Lily is the floral emblem of Saskatchewan, but it is becoming increasingly rare, owing to picking of the flower. The plants do not survive transplantation well, but can be grown from seeds, though the propagated plants might not flower for several years. The bulbs were eaten by some Native tribes, but were generally considered to be bitter. The Blackfoot treated spider bites with a wet dressing of the crushed flowers. This plant is often confused with Columbia Lily (*L. columbianum*), shown on page 267, also known as Tiger Lily, which is coloured similarly, but the petals on the Columbia Lily are curled backward, while the petals on the Wood Lily are held in a chalice-shape.

Mountain Hollyhock
Iliamna rivularis

MALLOW FAMILY

This large plant can grow up to 2 m tall, and appears in montane to subalpine elevations on moist slopes, stream banks, and meadows. The leaves are fairly large, alternate, irregularly toothed, and resemble maple leaves, with five to seven lobes each. The relatively large, pink to whitish, saucer-shaped flowers resemble garden Hollyhocks. They appear from the leaf axils along the stem and at the tips of the stems, in long, interrupted clusters. The flowers have many stamens, the filaments of which are united at the base to form a tube.

The derivation of the genus name, *Iliamna*, is unknown, though some authorities suggest that it honours Rhea Sylvia (also known as *Ilia*), the mythological mother of Romulus and Remus, the twins who are said to have founded Rome. The species name, *rivularis*, is derived from Latin and means "of the brook," a reference to the plant's favoured habitat. Mountain Hollyhock is an early succession plant following a forest fire. The plant also goes by two locally common names, Streambank Wild Hollyhock and Streambank Globe Mallow.

Showy Milkweed
Asclepias speciosa

MILKWEED FAMILY

This perennial plant is rather spectacular, with its tall, coarse stem, large leaves, and round clusters of pink to purple flowers. It grows up to 2 m tall from a thick, creeping rootstock, often occurring in clumps. It is found in moist grasslands, along roadsides, in thickets, and along streams. The leaves are dark green, opposite, short-stalked, oblong or oval, thick, prominently veined, and rounded at the tip, sometimes having a sharp spine. The flowers have a strong scent and occur in dense, rounded, umbrella-shaped clusters that can measure 7 cm across. Each flower is up to 1 cm long, and the corolla is five-parted, with reflexed lobes that have the appearance of horns that curve inward.

The genus name, *Asclepias*, honours Asklepios, the Greek god of medicine, perhaps a reference to the plant's supposed medicinal properties. The species name, *speciosa*, is Latin for "showy." The common name, Milkweed, arises because the plant exudes a milky latex when its stem is cut. Some Native peoples would gather this latex, allow it to harden, and then use it as a chewing gum. The plant contains alkaloids and resins in its stems and leaves which may cause it to be poisonous to livestock. The plant is a host plant to monarch butterflies, the larvae of which feed on it, and are said to accumulate the alkaloids as a defence mechanism against predators.

Wild Bergamot
Monarda fistulosa

MINT FAMILY

This showy flower inhabits grasslands and open woods, blooming in the summer months. The stems of the plant are erect and square, with a strong and distinctive odour of mint. The stem is topped by a dense cluster of pink to violet flowers. The leaves are opposite, triangular to ovate, and pointed at the ends.

The genus name, *Monarda*, honours 16th-century Spanish physician, Nicholas Monardez, who described many North American plants. The species name, *fistulosa*, means "tubular," a reference to the flower shape. Native peoples used Bergamot medicinally for various ailments, from acne, to bronchial complaints, to stomach pains. Some tribes used the plant as a perfume, meat preservative, and insect repellant. It is also reported that the plant was used ceremonially in the Sun Dance. Local common names include Horsemint, Bee Balm, and Oswego Tea.

Fairy Slipper (Venus Slipper)
Calypso bulbosa

ORCHID FAMILY

This orchid is found in shaded, moist coniferous forests. The flowers are solitary and nodding on leafless stems. The flower has pinkish to purplish sepals, and mauve side petals. The lip is whitish or purplish, with red to purple spots or stripes, and is hairy yellow inside. The flower is on the top of a single stalk, with a deeply wrinkled appearance. This small but extraordinarily beautiful flower blooms in the early spring, often occurring in colonies.

The Fairy Slipper has many common names, including Venus Slipper and Calypso Orchid. The genus name, *Calypso*, is derived from Greek mythology, Calypso being a daughter of Atlas. *Calypso* means "concealment," and is very apt, given that this flower is very easy to miss, being small, delicate, and growing in out-of-the-way places. The species name, *bulbosa*, refers to the bulb-like corm from which the flower grows. Do not attempt to transplant this flower. It needs specific fungi in the soil to grow successfully. Its range has diminished over time, owing to over-picking.

Spotted Coralroot (Summer Coralroot)
Corallorhiza maculata

ORCHID FAMILY

A plant of moist woods and bogs, this orchid grows from extensive coral-like rhizomes. There are no leaves, but the plant has several membranous bracts that sheath the purplish to brownish stem. A number of flowers appear on each stem, loosely arranged up the stem in a raceme. The three sepals and two upper petals are reddish purple. The lip petal is white, with dark red or purple spots and two lateral lobes. When sprouting in the spring, the plants resemble purple asparagus.

The genus name, *Corallorhiza*, is derived from the Greek *korallion*, meaning "coral," and *rhiza*, meaning "root," a reference to the coral-shaped rhizomes from which the plant grows. Lacking chlorophyll, this plant does not produce food by photosynthesis, but rather through parasitizing fungi in the soil. Several other Coralroots occur in the same habitat. Pale Coralroot (*C. trifida*) is yellow to yellow-greenish in colour; Striped Coralroot (*C. striata*) is pinkish to purplish and has vertical stripes on each sepal; Western Coralroot (*C. mertensiana*) is the least common in the region. It is similar in colour to Spotted Coralroot, but it lacks the spotting on the lip.

Red Clover
Trifolium pratense

PEA FAMILY

A European species now well established in North America, Red Clover grows to 60 cm tall in low to middle elevations. The leaves are in threes, often displaying a white crescent-shaped spot near the base. The flowers are pea-like, pinkish to purple, and up to 200 of them occur in a dense head, 2–3 cm in diameter, at stem tops. Two leaves lie immediately below the flower head.

All clovers have leaves in threes and flowers in dense heads. The name Clover is derived from the Latin *clava*, meaning "club," and more particularly the triple-headed cudgel carried by Hercules. That club bears a resemblance to the shape of the leaf on Clover. The suit of clubs in cards is from the same root, and has the same shape. White Clover (*T. repens*) is a similar plant in the same habitat. White Clover has a creeping stem and white to pinkish flowers on longer stalks. Herbalists favour Red Clover in the treatment of skin problems.

Scarlet Gilia (Skyrocket)
Ipomopsis aggregata (formerly *Gilia aggregata*)

PHLOX FAMILY

This plant is a biennial that occurs in semi-desert areas, on open rocky slopes, in dry meadows, grasslands, and open forests at low to moderately high elevations. In its first year, the plant puts out a rosette of basal leaves that are arranged pinnately into numerous narrow segments. The leaves emit a skunk-like odour when crushed. In the second year, the plant puts up one to several flowering stems up to 1 m tall which are sticky-hairy on the upper parts. The numerous flowers are clustered at the tops of the stems. The flowers are fiery red to reddish-orange to pink (often speckled with white), trumpet-shaped, up to 3 cm long, and each has five sharply pointed, spreading lobes.

There appears to be some dispute among the authorities as to origin of the genus name, *Ipomopsis*. One school of thought holds that the name means "similar to Morning Glories," while the other school opines that the name is derived from the Greek *ips*, which means "to strike," and *opsis*, which means "appearance," ergo "striking appearance," which certainly accurately describes the flower. The plant was once in the genus *Gilia*, named to honour 18th-century Italian clergyman and scientist Filippo Luigi Gilii, thus the origin of the common name. The specific name, *aggregata*, means "brought together," most probably a reference to the appearance of the inflorescence. The plant was first described for science in 1814 by Frederick Pursh from a specimen collected by Meriwether Lewis in June 1806 on the Lolo Trail in present-day Idaho.

Moss Campion
Silene acaulis

PINK FAMILY

This low-growing, ground-hugging cushion plant occupies an alpine environment in rock crevices, on cliffs, and exposed ridges. The bright green, narrow leaves are linear to narrowly lance-shaped, arise from the base of the plant, and often form cushions up to 1 m in diameter, resembling moss. Dead leaves from previous seasons often persist for years. The small, pink, five-lobed, tubular flowers are borne on single, short stalks, but they often appear to be sitting on the mossy surface.

The origin of the genus name, *Silene*, is discussed in the note on Night-Flowering Catchfly (*S. noctiflora*), shown on page 194. The species name, *acaulis*, means "not stalked," a reference to the stalkless appearance of the flowers. While this is an alpine species, it is often grown in rock gardens, and is easily propagated from seeds.

Bitterroot
Lewisia rediviva

PURSLANE FAMILY

A plant of rocky slopes, dry grasslands, and sagebrush slopes of the inter-mountain region, the Bitterroot was first catalogued by Captain Meriwether Lewis of the Lewis and Clark Expedition, and the genus is named for him. The strikingly beautiful flowers are deep pink to sometimes white, and have about 15 narrow petals. The flowers occur on such short stalks that they virtually appear to rest on the soil's surface. The flowers only open in the sun. The leaves are all basal, appearing in the spring but withering and receding into the ground prior to the flower blooming.

The Bitterroot was used as food and a trading item by many Plains Indian tribes, and, indeed, wars were fought over Bitterroot collection grounds. The roots were dug in the early spring, then peeled and cooked or dried for winter use. The members of the Lewis and Clark Expedition found the roots very bitter to the taste, hence the common name. Lewis first collected the root in present-day Montana in 1806. His pressed, dried specimen was shipped east for scrutiny, and when examined many months after collection it still showed signs of life. When planted, it promptly grew, giving it its species name, *rediviva*, meaning "restored to life." The Bitterroot River in Montana takes its name from the plant (having originally been named Clark's River), and the plant is the floral emblem of the State of Montana.

Dwarf Woodland Rose (Baldhip Rose)
Rosa gymnocarpa

ROSE FAMILY

Werner Eigelsreiter image

This is a slender, straggly shrub that grows to over 1 m tall in moist to dry woods and forest areas in the region. Its leaves are pinnately compound with five to nine elliptic, double-toothed leaflets that are 4 cm long. The plant is armed with numerous slender thorns. The flowers are the familiar pink wild roses, borne singly on short stems from the leaf axils, with golden stamens in the center of the spreading pink petals. The fruits are round, red, shiny rosehips that have no withered sepals attached.

The genus name requires no explanation. The species name, *gymnocarpa*, means "naked fruit," a reference to the rosehips that have no withered sepals attached. This is the only member of the genus that does not retain the withered sepals on the ripe fruits. Rosehips are rich in vitamin C and are a favourite food of many species of birds. They can also be used to make a wonderfully flavourful jelly. Native peoples used rose plants for medicinal purposes, and made fishing lures from the thorns.

Dwarf Raspberry (Arctic Blackberry)
Rubus arcticus (also *R. acaulis*)

ROSE FAMILY

This plant is a low, creeping, dwarf shrub that grows from a trailing rootstock, and is most often found in wet meadows and around seeps in the subalpine and alpine zones. The leaves are divided into three leaflets that are round to heart-shaped, and have coarsely toothed edges. The flowers are usually solitary, pink, and five-petalled. The fruits are clusters of red to purple drupelets, the aggregate of which is the raspberry. The fruits are small, but sweet and flavourful.

The genus name, *Rubus*, is the Latin name for brambles, from the root *rubra*, meaning "red," a reference to the colour of the fruits of many members of the genus. The berries have long been used as food, and some Native peoples used them to concoct a tea. The plant is also locally known as Dwarf Nagoonberry, but the origin of that name is unclear. One possible origin for that name is the Tlingit people of southern Alaska, where the plant is common. In the Tlingit language the fruit of this plant is called *neigoon*, which may have been Anglicized to nagoon.

Hardhack (Douglas' Spirea)
Spiraea douglasii

ROSE FAMILY

This is an erect, deciduous, freely branching shrub that forms dense, impenetrable thickets up to 2 m tall in marshy areas and along streams in low to middle elevations. The leaves are oblong, elliptic, 3–9 cm long, and notched at the tips. The inflorescence is a tall, elongated cluster of hundreds of tiny pink flowers. The flowers are relatively short-lived, quickly turning brown and drab in appearance.

The genus name, *Spiraea*, is from the Greek *speira*, which means "twisted," or "wound together," possibly a reference to plants of this genus being used as garlands. The species name honours the intrepid Scottish explorer and botanist David Douglas. The common name, Hardhack, is said to arise because the dense thickets of the plant are hard to hack through for hikers, loggers and any others who might try to move through an area where they grow. Ungulates browse the plants, and butterflies and bees are drawn to the flowers. The plant also has the locally common name of Steeplebush. Subalpine Spirea (*S. densiflora*), also called Pink Spirea by some, is a similar plant that occurs in subalpine areas in the region. It too has pink flowers, but they occur in a dense, flat-topped or rounded cluster.

Old Man's Whiskers (Three-Flowered Avens)
Geum triflorum

ROSE FAMILY

This plant is widespread on dry plateaus at low to subalpine elevations, open grasslands, and arid basins in the region. The flowers bloom in early spring, and are dull purplish to pinkish, hairy, and nodding at the top of the stem. The flowers usually occur in a cluster of 3, though some plants will have as many as five flowers on a single stem. The flowers remain semi-closed and do not open out flat. They were once described to me as "looking like three very tired ballerinas at the close of a performance." The fruits are a feathery cluster of plume-like brownish to purplish achenes.

The origin of the genus name, *Geum*, is discussed in the note on Large-Leaved Avens (*G. macrophyllum*), shown on page 55. The specific name, *triflorum*, refers to the three flowers that are typical in this species. The common name Old Man's Whiskers is a reference to the appearance of the fruits that resemble grey whiskers. These fruits are distributed by winds, and it is said that they sometimes occurred in such abundance on the unbroken prairies that when the seeds blew, it looked like smoke over the prairies, hence another common name, Prairie Smoke. Some Native peoples boiled the roots to make a tea to use as a medicine for colds, flu, and fever.

Prickly Rose
Rosa acicularis

ROSE FAMILY

This is a deciduous shrub that grows up to 1.5 m tall, with freely branched stems and thorns at the base of each leaf. The flowers are pink with five broad petals. Leaves are oblong and notched, somewhat hairy below. The Prickly Rose will easily hybridize with other members of the Rose Family, and the hybrids can be difficult to specifically identify. The fruits are dark red, fleshy, round to oval hips with sepals remaining on top, like a beard. They are rich in vitamin C, and can be a favourite food of many species of birds. The hips can be used to make a delicious jelly.

The foliage and young stems of wild roses are browsed by wild ungulates and domestic livestock. Native peoples used the plants extensively for a wide variety of purposes – medicinally, as food, for fibre for cordage, and for making fishing lures from the thorns. Wild roses produce root suckers, and can be very invasive and aggressive in spreading. This plant is the floral emblem of the Province of Alberta. Nootka Rose (*R. nutkana*) is a similar rose that occurs in the region. It tends to have larger flowers than other wild roses, and it usually favours wooded areas at higher elevations.

Roseroot
Sedum integrifolium

STONECROP FAMILY

This plant occurs in the subalpine and alpine zones, favouring moist rocky scree, talus, and ridges. The stems arise from a fleshy rootstock, and they are covered in persistent leaves. The leaves are oval to oblong, fleshy, and somewhat flattened. The flowers have oblong petals, are rose-coloured to purple, and occur in rounded, flat-topped, dense clusters atop the stems.

The origin of the genus name, *Sedum*, is discussed in the note on Lance-Leaved Stonecrop (*S. lanceolatum*), shown on page 62. The species name, *integrifolia*, indicates that the leaf margins are entire and not cut or toothed. When the roots are cut or bruised, they give off the fragrance of roses, thus the common name. Another common name is King's Crown, a reference to the shape of the inflorescence. Some Native peoples used Roseroot medicinally in poultices.

Glossary

Achene: A dry, single-seeded fruit that does not split open at maturity.

Alkaloid: Any of a group of complex, nitrogen-based chemicals, often found in plants, that are thought to protect the plants against insect predation. Many of these substances are poisonous.

Alternate: A reference to the arrangement of leaves on a stem where the leaves appear singly and staggered on opposite sides of the stem.

Annual: A plant that completes its life cycle, from seed germination to production of new seed, within one year, and then dies.

Anther: The portion of the stamen (the male portion of a flower) that produces pollen.

Axil: The upper angle formed where a leaf, branch, or other organ is attached to a plant stem.

Basal: A reference to leaves where the leaves are found at the base or bottom of the plant, usually near or on the ground.

Berry: A fleshy, many-seeded fruit.

Biennial: A plant that completes its life cycle in two years, normally producing leaves in the first year but not producing flowers until the second year, and then dies.

Bilabiate: In reference to floral construction, having two lips.

Blade: The body of a leaf, excluding the stalk.

Bract: A reduced or otherwise modified leaf that is usually found near the flower or inflorescence of a plant but is not part of the flower or inflorescence.

Bristle: A stiff hair, usually erect or curving away from its attachment point.

Bulb: An underground plant part derived from a short, often rounded shoot that is covered with scales or leaves.

Calcareous: In reference to soils, containing calcium carbonate.

Calyx: The outer set of flower parts, usually composed of sepals.

Capsule: A dry fruit with more than one compartment that splits open to release seeds.

Clasping: In reference to a leaf, surrounding or partially wrapping around a stem or branch.

Cluster: A grouping or close arrangement of individual flowers that is not dense and continuous.

Composite inflorescence: A flower-like inflorescence of the Composite Family, composed of ray and/or disk flowers. Where both ray and disk flowers are present, the ray flowers surround the disk flowers.

Compound leaf: A leaf that is divided into two or many leaflets, each of which may look like a complete leaf, but which lacks buds. Compound leaves may have a variety of arrangements. Pinnate leaves have leaflets arranged like a feather, with attachment to a central stem. Palmate leaves have leaflets radiating from a common point, like the fingers of a hand.

Connate: In reference to leaves, where two leaves are fused at their bases to form a shallow cup, often seen in the Honeysuckle Family.

Corm: An enlarged base or stem resembling a bulb.

Corolla: The collective term for the petals of the flower that are found inside the sepals.

Cultivar: A cultivated variety of a wild plant.

Cyme: A broad, flat-topped flower arrangement in which the inner, central flowers bloom first.

Decumbent: In reference to a plant, reclining or lying on the ground, with tip ascending.

Disk flower: Any of the small tubular florets found in the central clustered portion of the flower head of members of the Composite Family; also referred to as "disk florets."

Dioecious: Having unisex flowers, where male and female flowers appear on separate plants. See also **monoecious**.

Drupe: A fleshy or juicy fruit that covers a single, stony seed inside, e.g., a cherry or peach.

Drupelet: Any one part of an aggregate fruit, e.g., a raspberry or a blackberry, where each such part is a fleshy fruit that covers a single, stony seed inside.

Elliptic: Ellipse-shaped, widest in the middle.

Elongate: Having a slender form, long in relation to width.

Entire: In reference to a leaf, a leaf edge that is smooth, without teeth or notches.

Filament: The part of the stamen that supports the anther. Also can refer to any threadlike structure.

Florescence: Generally the flowering part of a plant; the arrangement of the flowers on the stem; also referred to as "inflorescence."

Floret: One of the small tubular flowers in the central clustered portion of the flower head of members of the Composite Family; also known as "disk flower."

Flower head: A dense and continuous group of flowers without obvious branches or spaces between.

Follicle: A dry fruit composed of a single compartment that splits open along one side at maturity to release seeds.

Fruit: The ripe ovary with the enclosed seeds, and any other structures that enclose it.

Glabrous: In reference to a leaf surface, smooth, neither waxy or sticky.

Gland: A small organ that secrets a sticky or oily substance and is attached to some part of the plant.

Glandular hairs: Small hairs attached to glands on plants.

Glaucous: Having a fine, waxy, often white coating that may be rubbed off; often characteristic of leaves, fruits, and stems.

Hood: In reference to flower structure, a curving or folded, petal-like structure interior to the petals and exterior to the stamens in certain flowers.

Host: In reference to a parasitic or semi-parasitic plant, the plant from which the parasite obtains its nourishment.

Inflorescence: Generally the flowering part of a plant; the arrangement of the flowers on the stem; also referred to as "florescence."

Involucral bract: A modified leaf found just below an inflorescence.

Keel: A ridge or fold, shaped like the bottom of a boat, which may refer to leaf structure, or more often to the two fused petals in flowers that are members of the Pea Family.

Lanate: Covered with woolly hair.

Lance-shaped: In reference to leaf shape, much longer than wide, widest below the middle and tapering to the tip, like the blade of a lance.

Leaflet: A distinct, leaflike segment of a compound leaf.

Linear: Like a line; long, narrow, and parallel-sided.

Lobe: A reference to the arrangement of leaves; a segment of a divided plant part, typically rounded.

Margin: The edge of a leaf or petal.

Mat: A densely interwoven or tangled, low, ground-hugging growth.

Midrib: The main rib of a leaf.

Midvein: The middle vein of a leaf.

Monoecious: A plant having unisex flowers, with separate male and female flowers on the same plant. See also **dioecious**.

Nectary: A plant structure that produces and secretes nectar.

Node: A joint on a stem or root.

Noxious weed: A plant, usually imported, that out-competes with and drives out native plants.

Oblong: Somewhat rectangular, with rounded ends.

Obovate: Shaped like a teardrop.

Opposite: A reference to the arrangement of leaves on a stem where the leaves appear paired on opposite sides of the stem, directly across from each other. See also **palmate**, **pinnate**.

Oval: Broadly elliptic.

Ovary: The portion of the flower where the seeds develop. It is usually a swollen area below the style and stigma.

Ovate: Egg shaped.

Palmate: A reference to the arrangement of leaves on a stem where the leaves spread like the fingers on a hand, diverging from a central or common point. See also **pinnate, opposite**.

Panicle: A branched inflorescence that blooms from the bottom up.

Pappus: The cluster of bristles, scales, or hairs at the top of an achene in the flowers of the Composite Family.

Pencilled: Marked with coloured lines, like the petals on Violets.

Perennial: A plant that does not produce seeds or flowers until its second year of life, then lives for three or more years, usually flowering each year, before dying.

Petal: A component of the inner floral portion of a flower, often the most brightly coloured and visible part of the flower.

Petiole: The stem of a leaf.

Pinnate: A reference to the arrangement of leaves on a stem where the leaves appear in two rows on opposite sides of a central stem, similar to the construction of a feather. See also **opposite**, **palmate**.

Pistil: The female member of a flower that produces seed, consisting of the ovary, the style, and the stigma. A flower may have one to several separate pistils.

Pistillate: A flower with female reproductive parts but no male reproductive parts.

Pod: A dry fruit.

Pollen: The tiny, often powdery, male reproductive microspores formed in the stamens and necessary for sexual reproduction in flowering plants.

Pome: A fruit with a core, e.g., an apple or pear.

Prickle: A small, sharp, spiny outgrowth from an outer surface.

Raceme: A flower arrangement that has an elongated flower cluster with the flowers attached to short stalks of relatively equal length that are attached to the main central stalk.

Ray flower: One of the outer strap-shaped petals seen in members of the Composite Family. Ray flowers may surround disk flowers or may comprise the whole of the flower head; also referred to as "ray florets."

Receptacle: The enlarged end of a stem to which the flower parts – ray and disk flowers – are attached in members of the Composite Family.

Reflexed: Bent backward, often in reference to petals, bracts, or stalks.

Rhizome: An underground stem that produces roots and shoots at the nodes.

Riverine: Moist habitats along rivers or streams.

Rootstock: Short, erect underground stem from which new leaves and shoots are produced annually.

Rosette: A dense cluster of basal leaves from a common underground part, often in a flattened, circular arrangement.

Runner: A long, trailing, or creeping stem.

Saprophyte: An organism that obtains its nutrients from dead organic matter.

Scape: A flowering stem, usually leafless, rising from the crown, roots, or corm of a plant. Scapes can have a single or many flowers.

Sepal: A leaf-like appendage that surrounds the petals of a flower. Collectively the sepals make up the calyx.

Serrate: Possessing sharp, forward-pointing teeth.

Sessile: Of leaves, attached directly to the base, without a stalk.

Shrub: A multi-stemmed, woody plant.

Simple leaf: A leaf that has a single leaf-like blade, which may be lobed, or divided.

Spike: An elongated, unbranched cluster of stalkless or nearly stalkless flowers.

Spine: A thin, stiff, sharp-pointed projection.

Spur: A hollow, tubular projection arising from the base of a petal or sepal, often producing nectar.

Spurred corolla: A corolla that has spurs.

Stalk: The stem supporting the leaf, flower, or flower cluster.

Stamen: The male member of the flower that produces pollen, typically consisting of an anther and a filament.

Staminate: A flower with male reproductive parts but no female reproductive parts.

Staminode: A sterile stamen.

Standard: The uppermost petal of a typical flower in the Pea Family.

Stigma: The portion of the pistil receptive to pollination; usually at the top of the style, and often sticky or fuzzy.

Stipule: An appendage, usually in pairs, found at the base of a leaf or leaf stalk.

Stolon: A creeping, above-ground stem capable of sending up a new plant.

Style: A slender stalk connecting the stigma to the ovary in the female organ of a flower.

Talus: Loose, fragmented rock rubble usually found at the base of a rock wall; also known as "scree."

Taproot: A stout main root that extends downward.

Tendril: A slender, coiled, or twisted filament with which climbing plants attach to their supports.

Tepals: Petals and sepals that cannot be distinguished from one another.

Terminal: At the top of, such as of a stem or other appendage.

Terminal flower head: A flower that appears at the top of a stem, as opposed to originating from a leaf axil.

Ternate: Arranged in threes, often in reference to leaf structures.

Toothed: Bearing teeth or sharply angled projections along the edge.

Trailing: Lying flat on the ground but not rooting.

Tuber: A thick, creeping underground stem.

Tubular: Hollow or cylindrical, usually in reference to a fused corolla.

Umbel: A flower arrangement where the flower stalks have a common point of attachment to the stem, like the spokes of an umbrella.

Unisexual: Some flowers are unisexual, having either male parts or female parts but not both. Some plants are unisexual, having either male flowers or female flowers but not both.

Urn-shaped: Hollow and cylindrical or globular, contracted at the mouth; like an urn.

Vacuole: A membrane-bound compartment in a plant that is typically filled with liquid and may perform various functions in the plant.

Vein: A small tube that carries water, nutrients, and minerals, usually in reference to leaves.

Viscid: Sticky, thick, and gluey.

Whorl: Three or more parts attached at the same point along a stem or axis, often surrounding the stem; forming a ring radiating out from a common point.

Wings: Side petals that flank the keel in typical flowers of the Pea Family.

Photographic Credits

All photographs are by the author except those listed below, with sincere thanks by the author to the photographers for their gracious permission to use their work in this book.

Werner Eigelsreiter
Dwarf Woodland Rose p. 280
Large-Flowered Collomia p. 51

Anne Elliott
Fringed Loosestrife p. 52

Dave Ingram
Mist Maiden p. 224

Jim Riley
Buck-Bean p. 111

Gill Ross
Bracted Lousewort p. 32
Western St. John's Wort p. 61

Doug Skilton
White Dryad p. 207
Black Huckleberry Fruit p. 254

Virginia Skilton
Alaska Rein-Orchid p. 180
Blazing Star p. 5
Broad-Leaved Arrowhead p. 223
Clustered Broomrape p. 110
Creamy Peavine p. 189
Curly-Cup Gumweed p. 18
Lingonberry p. 150
Mountain Marsh Marigold p. 118
Shrubby Penstemon p. 83
Sibbaldia p. 57
Sulphur Lupine p. 49
Western Tea Berry p. 154
   (both images)
Yellow Rattle p. 37

Tracy Utting
Purple Saxifrage p. 103

BIBLIOGRAPHY

Clark, L.J. and J. Trelawny (ed.), 1973, 1976, 1998. *Wildflowers of the Pacific Northwest.* Harbour Publishing, Madeira Park, British Columbia.

Cormack, R.G.H., 1977. *Wild Flowers of Alberta.* Hurtig Publishers, Edmonton, Alberta.

Kershaw, L., A. MacKinnon and J. Pojar, 1998. *Plants of the Rocky Mountains.* Lone Pine Publishing, Edmonton, Alberta.

Parish, R., R. Coupé, and D. Lloyd (eds.), 1996. *Plants of Southern Interior British Columbia.* Lone Pine Publishing, Edmonton, Alberta.

Phillips, H.W., 2001. *Northern Rocky Mountain Wildflowers.* Falcon Publishing Inc., Helena, Montana.

Phillips, H.W., 2003. *Plants of the Lewis & Clark Expedition.* Mountain Press Publishing Co., Missoula, Montana.

Scotter, G.W., H. Flygare, 1986. *Wildflowers of the Canadian Rockies.* Hurtig Publishers Ltd., Edmonton, Alberta.

Vance, F.R., J.R. Jowsey, J.S. McLean, and F.A.Switzer, 1999. *Wildflowers across the Prairies.* Greystone Books, Vancouver, British Columbia.

Wilkinson, K. 1999. *Wildflowers of Alberta.* University of Alberta Press and Lone Pine Publishing, Edmonton, Alberta.

INDEX

A

Acer glabrum, 42
Achillea millefolium, 136
Aconitum columbianum, 75
Actaea rubra, 116
Adenocaulon bicolor, 134
Agoseris aurantiaca, 238
Alaska Rein-Orchid, 180
Alaska Saxifrage, 210
Alfalfa, 96
Allium cernuum, 268
Alnus crispa ssp. *sinuata*,
    109
    viridis ssp. *sinuata*, 109
Alpine Bistort, 113
Alpine Forget-Me-Not, 68
Alpine Harebell, 88
Alpine Speedwell, 81
Alpine Spring Beauty, 196
Alpine Veronica, 81
Alpine Willowherb, 246
Amelanchier alnifolia, 203
Amerorchis rotundifolia,
    185
Anaphalis margaritacea,
    135
Anemone multifida, 234
    occidentalis, 120
    patens, 76
Angelica arguta, 126
Annual Hawksbeard, 25
Antelope Brush, 53
Antennaria microphylla,
    240
    rosea, 240
*Apocynum androsaemifo-
    lium*, 244
Apocynum cannabinum,
    244
    medium, 244
Aquilegia flavescens, 11, 232
    formosa, 232
Arabis drummondii, 178
    holboellii, 178
    lyallii, 178
Aralia nudicaulis, 145
Arctic Blackberry, 281

Arctium minus, 237
Arctostaphylos uva-ursi, 253
Arnica cordifolia, 22
    latifolia, 22
Arrow-Leaved Balsam-
    root, 15
Arrow-Leaved Ground-
    sel, 28
Arrow-Leaved Sweet Colts-
    foot, 129
Artemisia spp, 110
Arumleaf Arrowhead, 223
Asarum caudatum, 227
Asclepias speciosa, 272
Aster conspicuus, 79
Autumn Dwarf Gentian, 86

B

Baldhip Rose, 280
Ballhead Waterleaf, 105
Balsamorhiza sagittata, 15
Baneberry, 116
Bare-Stemmed Mitrewort,
    211
Bastard Toadflax, 209
Beadlily, 168
Bearberry, 45, 253
Beardtongue, 84
Beargrass, 161
Beaver Poison, 128
Bee Balm, 273
Belgium Endive, 78
Bell-Bind, 176
Berberis nervosa, 3
Bigseed Biscuitroot, 124
Bilberry, 257
Birch-Leaf Spirea, 197
Bird Vetch, 99
Birth Root, 172
Bishop's Cap, 211
Bitterbrush, 53
Bitterroot, 279
Black Elderberry, 157
Black Gooseberry, 242
Black Hawthorn, 198
Black Huckleberry, 254
Black Medick, 96
Black Sanicle, 13
Black Snakeroot, 13
Black Twinberry, 39

Bladder Locoweed, 97
Blazing Star, 5
Blue Clematis, 73
Blue Devil, 69
Blue Elderberry, 157
Blue Flax, 85
Blue Lettuce, 77
Blue Sailors, 78
Blue Star, 89
Bluebead Lily, 168
Blue-Eyed Grass, 89
Blueweed (Viper's
    Bugloss), 69
Blunt-Leaved Orchid, 184
Bog Cranberry, 255
Bog-Bean, 111
Bracted Honeysuckle, 39
Bracted Lousewort, 32
Brittle Prickly-Pear Cactus,
    12
Broadleaf Arrowead, 223
Broad-Leaved Arnica, 22
Broad-Leaved Arrowhead,
    223
Broad-Leaved Stonecrop,
    62
Broad-Leaved Willowherb,
    246
Bronzebells, 162
Brown-Eyed Susan, 16
Buck-Bean, 111
Bull Thistle, 235
Bunchberry, 139
Butter and Eggs, 33
Butterweed, 30
Butterwort, 67
Button Flowers, 29

C

Calochortus apiculatus, 171
    lyallii, 171
    macrocarpus, 269
Caltha leptosepala, 118
Calypso bulbosa, 274
Calypso Orchid, 274
Calystegia arvensis, 176
    sepium, 176
Camassia quamash, 91
Campanula lasiocarpa, 88
    rotundifolia, 88

Neil Jennings is an ardent fly fisher, hiker, and photographer who loves "getting down in the dirt" pursuing his keen interest in wildflowers.

For 22 years he was a co-owner of Country Pleasures, a fly-fishing retailer in Calgary, Alberta. He fly fishes extensively, in both fresh and salt water, and his angling pursuits usually lead him to wildflower investigations in a variety of venues. He has taught fly-fishing-related courses in Calgary for over 20 years, and his photographs and writings on the subject have appeared in a number of outdoor magazines. Neil has previously written three books on western wildflowers – *Uncommon Beauty*, *Alpine Beauty*, and *Prairie Beauty* – all published by Rocky Mountain Books. He is also the author of *Behind the Counter*, a book on fly fishing, also published by Rocky Mountain Books. Neil lives in Calgary with Linda, his wife of over 30 years. They spend a lot of time outdoors together chasing fish, flowers, and, as often as possible, grandchildren.

Coastal Beauty

Wildflowers and flowering Shrubs of Coastal
British Columbia and Vancouver Island

By Neil L. Jennings

Coastal Beauty explores the wildflowers and flowering
shrubs commonly found in the coastal regions of British
Columbia, including Vancouver Island, and also Coastal
Washington and Oregon.

ISBN: 978-1-897522-02-8
Price: $26.95
Pages: 304 pages. 5" x 8". Paperback
Illustrations: colour photos throughout

Alpine Beauty

Alpine and Subalpine Wildflowers of the
Canadian Rockies and Columbia Mountains

By Neil L. Jennings

Alpine Beauty explores the wildflowers and flowering shrubs
commonly found in the subalpine and alpine environments in
the Rocky Mountains of western Canada. Due to harsh weather
conditions, the plants that exist at higher elevations are generally
different than those at lower elevations. In this environment,
low shrub and herb communities become the rule.

ISBN: 978-1-894765-83-1
Price: $22.95
Pages: 224 pages. 5" x 8". Paperback
Illustrations: colour photos throughout

Uncommon Beauty

Wildflowers and Flowering Shrubs of Southern
Alberta and Southeastern British Columbia

By Neil L. Jennings

Uncommon Beauty explores the wildflowers and
flowering shrubs of a large area from Jasper down to
Creston, over to Glacier National Park in Montana,
and up through Lethbridge and Edmonton.

ISBN: 978-1-894765-75-6
Price: $22.95
Pages: 256 pages. 5" x 8". Paperback
Illustrations: colour photos throughout

Prairie Beauty

Wildflowers of the Canadian Prairies

By Neil L. Jennings

Prairie Beauty explores the wildflowers and flowering shrubs commonly found in the prairie environment of western Canada.

ISBN: 978-1-894765-84-8
Price: $24.95
Pages: 248 pages. 5" x 8". Paperback
Illustrations: colour photos throughout

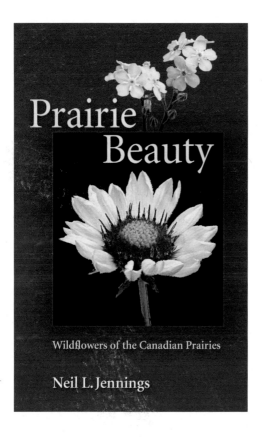